THE PSALTER

THE PSALTER

A faithful and inclusive rendering

from the Hebrew into contemporary English

poetry, intended primarily for communal song and recitation.

This translation is offered for study and for comment by the

International Commission on English in the Liturgy.

◆

LTP

LITURGY TRAINING PUBLICATIONS

ACKNOWLEDGMENTS

The International Commission on English in the Liturgy (ICEL) acknowledges with gratitude the editorial committee and the subcommittee and its consultants who have ably and generously assisted at various stages of this project. It should be noted that some of the subcommittee members served for as many as 14 years. ICEL also thanks those parishes, religious communities, liturgical commissions and individuals who sent comments as the work progressed.

EDITORIAL COMMITTEE

Lawrence Boadt, CSP
Mary Collins, OSB
John Dzieglewicz, SJ
Peter Finn
Joseph Wimmer, OSA

SUBCOMMITTEE MEMBERS AND CONSULTANTS

Peter Barry
Lawrence Boadt, CSP
Rita Burns
Daniel Coughlin
Mary Collins, OSB
Margaret Daly
John Dzieglewicz, SJ
Peter Finn
Leslie Hoppe, OFM
Roderick MacKenzie, SJ
Mary McGann, RSCJ
John McGuckin
Marjorie Moffatt, SNJM

Joseph Mulrooney
Irene Nowell, OSB
James Schellman
Eileen Schuller, OSU
Geoffrey Boulton Smith
Pamela Stotter
Carroll Stuhlmueller, CP
Michael Suarez, SJ
Francis Sullivan, SJ
Thomas Troeger
Elizabeth-Anne Vanek
Christopher Willcock, SJ
Joseph Wimmer, OSA

The English translation of the *Liturgical Psalter* © 1994, International Committee on English in the Liturgy, Inc. All rights reserved. Reprinted with permission.

IMPRIMATUR

In accord with canon 825, §1 of the Code of Canon Law, the National Conference of Catholic Bishops hereby approves for publication the *Liturgical Psalter,* a translation of the Psalms submitted by the International Commission on English in the Liturgy.

> William Cardinal Keeler, D.D., J.C.D.
> President, National Conference of Catholic Bishops
> Washington, D.C., January 5, 1995

Editor: Gabe Huck. Editorial assistant: Jennifer McGeary. Art: Linda Ekstrom. Design: Kerry Perlmutter. Psalm introductory lines: Irene Nowell, Anne Marie Sweet, Elizabeth-Anne Vanek. Afterword: Staff of the International Commission on English in the Liturgy

Copyright © 1995, Archdiocese of Chicago: Liturgy Training Publications, 1800 North Hermitage Avenue, Chicago IL 60622-1101; 1-800-933-1800; FAX 1-800-933-7094. All rights reserved.

Library of Congress Cataloging-in-Publication Data
  The Psalter: a faithful and inclusive rendering from the Hebrew into contemporary English poetry, intended primarily for communal song and recitation . . . / offered for study and for comment by the International Commission on English in the Liturgy: [art, Linda Ekstrom]. 392 p.
    1. Psalters — Texts. 2. Catholic Church — Liturgy — Texts. 3. Bible. O.T. Psalms — Liturgical use. I. Ekstrom, Linda. II. International Committee on English in the Liturgy.
  BX2033.P72 1994
  264'.028 — dc   20 93-29361
                                         CIP

ISBN 0-929650-77-8 [casebound]   C/150P
ISBN 0-929650-88-3 [paper]   P/150P

v

CONTENTS

FOREWORD
Gabe Huck

What are the prayers of Jews? Of Christians? What is the sound and texture and tempo of Jews praying? Of Christians praying? The generations in all their scattered places have made the answers to such questions vast. Yet the indispensable core to those answers is remarkably simple. Jews have prayed and do pray the psalms. Christians have prayed and do pray the psalms. The sounds and the textures and the tempos of their prayer are the sounds and the textures and the tempos of the psalms.

The psalms are the river of the synagogue's prayer, of the church's prayer. Whatever else is said and done, it is said and done to the flowing of this river. Through the generations, the thanking, praising, cursing and lamenting of the psalms have shaped the vocabulary of synagogue and church. This chanting is joined in the public times and echoed in the households and the private spaces. Daybreak and awakening are marked with psalms as are day's end and night's rest. For Christians, the singing of the church—in every sort of rhythm from Byzantine chanting to the spirituals to the chorales—has drawn abundantly from these psalms.

This book is offered as the labor of scholars and artists to fashion a psalter for assemblies to sing and individuals to recite. Those who have prepared these texts have struggled for fidelity to the Hebrew texts and for the words and cadences of contemporary poetry. Their work intends to be in continuity with the English translations we have known until now, but it is clearly something new. Speak it, listen to it. If it has strength, if it has validity, that will emerge only with familiarity. Only when one begins to know some of these texts by heart will they be tested and proved. That is the nature of such speech.

Both those who are just now discovering the psalms and those who know them well will find much that is helpful in the essay by Carroll Stuhlmueller which follows Psalm 150. Stuhlmueller, a scholar who wrote widely on the psalms and who died while this volume was in preparation, discusses the structure of the Book of Psalms and the great spectrum of expression we can expect there.

The origin, goals and working process for this translation of the psalms are discussed in the Afterword. The work of the translators was completed in 1993. Following that, the text was submitted to the United States Bishops' Committee on Doctrine for the imprimatur. At that point the text was entirely free of gender-exclusive pronouns for God. Before the imprimatur was granted, however, the committee insisted that the translators use male pronouns for God in a very few places. The intention of the International Commission on English in the Liturgy is that this text be evaluated and revised before the end of the 1990s. The comments of all who use this translation are welcome and should be directed to the publisher at the address found on the acknowledgment pages.

To assist the reader, each psalm is prefaced by a brief summary line prepared for this edition. In many cases, this is followed by those notes and instructions that, while not a part of the poetry, have traditionally introduced the verses of the psalm. The divisions into stanzas and the groupings of the stanzas are the work of those who prepared the translation.

The psalms have been the prayers and the teachers of prayer for Jews and Christians. This book in its words, its art and its design hopes only to be at the service of that prayer.

1

**THE DISCIPLE DELIGHTS IN GOD'S WORD
AND IS ROOTED IN GOD'S TEACHING.
FLOURISH AND BEAR ABUNDANT FRUIT.**

---

1 If you would be happy:
 never walk with the wicked,
 never stand with sinners,
 never sit among cynics,
2 but delight in the Lord's teaching
 and study it night and day.

3 You will stand like a tree
 planted by a stream,
 bearing fruit in season,
 its leaves never fading,
 its yield always plenty.

◆

4 Not so for the wicked,
 like chaff they are blown by the wind.
5 They will not withstand the judgment,
 nor assemble with the just.
6 The Lord marks the way of the upright,
 but the corrupt walk to ruin. □

2

---

1 Why this strife among nations?
Why this pointless scheming?
2 Kings stand against God,
nobles plot together
against the Lord's anointed:
3 "Let us break these fetters,
let us cast off these chains!"

4 High above the earth
God laughs in mockery,
5 speaking in anger,
striking them with terror:
6 "On Zion, my holy mountain,
I anoint my king."

7 I repeat the Lord's decree:
"You are my son,
today I give you birth.
8 Ask and the nations are yours,
even the far-off lands.
9 You will strike them with an iron rod,
shatter them like clay pots."

10 Kings, come to your senses;
rulers, take heed.
11 Serve the Lord with joy,

tremble in awe,
bow at God's feet,
12 for if you provoke God's anger,
you will perish in a flash.
How much better
to find shelter in God! □

3

**A MORNING PRAYER.
WITH GOD AS PROTECTOR,
HUMAN OPPOSITION COUNTS FOR NOTHING.
SLEEP WELL AND AWAKE IN CONFIDENCE.**

*1 A psalm of David,
when he fled from his son Absalom.*

◆

2 Lord, how daunting the armies
massed against me!
3 All of them jeer at me,
"God will not save you."

◆

4 But you are my shield, Lord,
  my reason to boast;
  you hold my head high.
5 When I call, you answer
  from your holy mountain.

6 I rest easy at night
  and rise in the morning
  sure of God's protection.
7 I do not fear thousands
  standing against me.

◆

8 Rise up, Lord,
  rescue me, my God.
  Break their evil jaws!
  Smash their teeth!
9 Favor your people, Lord,
  for the victory is yours.   □

4

*1 For the choirmaster. For stringed instruments.
A psalm of David.*

◆

2 Answer when I call, faithful God.
You cleared away my trouble;
be good to me, listen to my prayer.

◆

3 How long, proud fools,
will you insult my honor,
loving lies and chasing shadows?
4 Look! God astounds believers,
the Lord listens when I call.

5 Tremble, but do not despair.
Attend to your heart,
be calm through the night,
6 worship with integrity,
trust in the Lord.

◆

7 Cynics ask, "Who will bless us?
　Even God has turned away."
8 You give my heart more joy
　than all their grain and wine.
9 I sleep secure at night,
　you keep me in your care.　☐

5

A MORNING PRAYER.
RELY ON GOD IN TIME OF NEED.
LIVE HUMBLY IN GOD'S PRESENCE.

---

1 *For the choirmaster. For wind instruments.*
A psalm of David.

◆

2 Hear my words, my groans,
3 my cries for help,
　O God my king.
4 I pray to you, Lord,
　my prayer rises with the sun.
　At dawn I plead my case and wait.

◆

5 You never welcome evil, God,
   never let it stay.
6 You hate arrogance
   and abhor scoundrels,
7 you detest violence
   and destroy the traitor.

◆

8 But by your great mercy
   I enter your house
   and bend low in awe
   within your holy temple.

9 In the face of my enemies
   clear the way,
   bring me your justice.

10 Their charges are groundless,
   they breathe destruction;
   their tongues are smooth,
   their throat an open grave.

11 God, pronounce them guilty,
   catch them in their own plots,
   expel them for their sins;
   they have betrayed you.

◆

12 But let those who trust you
be glad and celebrate for ever.
Protect those who love your name,
then they will delight in you.

13 For you bless the just, O God,
your grace surrounds them like a shield. □

6

WHEN PATIENCE IS EXPENDED,
ENERGY EXHAUSTED,
TRUST IN GOD'S MERCY.
PRAY FOR GOD'S DELIVERANCE.

*1 For the choirmaster.
For stringed instruments: upon the "eighth."
A psalm of David.*

2 Stop rebuking me, Lord,
hold back your rage.
3 Have pity, for I am spent;
heal me, hurt to the bone,
4 wracked to the limit.
Lord, how long? How long?

5 Repent, Lord, save me.
   You promised; keep faith!
6 In death, who remembers you?
   In Sheol, who gives you thanks?

7 Night after night I lie exhausted,
   hollow-eyed with grief,
8 my pillow soaked with tears:
   all because of my foes.

9 Get away, from me, scoundrels!
   The Lord has heard my tears.
10 God hears my pleading
   and will answer my prayer.
11 My foes will be shamed, shocked,
   turned back in sudden panic.   □

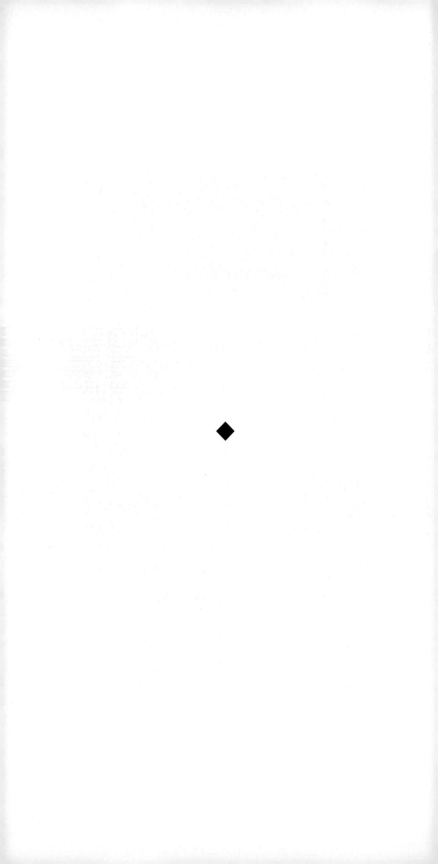

7

*1 A lamentation of David,
which he sang to the Lord
concerning Cush, the Benjaminite.*

◆

2 You are my haven, Lord my God,
   save me from my attackers.
3 Rescue me, their helpless prey;
   these lions will tear me to pieces.

◆

4 Lord, if I have done wrong,
   if there is guilt on my hands,
5 if I have mistreated friend or foe
   for no good reason,
6 then let the enemy hound me,
   overtake and kill me,
   trample me into the ground.

◆

7 Wake up, Lord!
Arise and rage
against my angry foes.
Provide the justice you demand.
8 Make the world a courtroom
and take your seat as judge.

9 Then, judge of all nations,
give me justice.
I have done what is right,
I am innocent.

10 Put an end to evil,
uphold the good;
you test our hearts,
God of right and truth.

◆

11 God who saves the honest
defends me like a shield.
12 God is a zealous judge
ready to say "guilty" every day
13 if sinners do not turn around.

Instead they sharpen their swords,
string their bows,
14 and light flaming arrows,
taking up lethal weapons.

psalm 7

◆

15 See how they conceive evil,
   grow pregnant with trouble,
   and give birth to lies.

16 Sinners land in the pit
   dug with their own hands.
17 Their evil crashes on their heads;
   they are victims of their own violence.

◆

18 I praise God who is right and good,
   I sing out, "Lord Most High!" □

8

A HYMN OF PRAISE.
INFANTS AND STARS
AND ALL CREATION SING PRAISE.
MARVEL IN GOD'S GLORY AND JOIN THIS SONG.

---

1 For the choirmaster. Upon the gittith.
A psalm of David.

2 Lord our God,
   the whole world tells
   the greatness of your name.
   Your glory reaches
   beyond the stars.

3 Even the babble of infants
   declares your strength,
   your power to halt
   the enemy and avenger.

4 I see your handiwork
   in the heavens:
   the moon and the stars
   you set in place.

5 What is humankind
   that you remember them,

the human race
that you care for them?

◆

6 You treat them like gods,
 dressing them in glory and splendor.
7 You give them charge of the earth,
 laying all at their feet:

8 cattle and sheep,
 wild beasts,
9 birds of the sky,
 fish of the sea,
 every swimming creature.

10 Lord our God,
 the whole world tells
 the greatness of your name.   □

9

*1 For the choirmaster. According to "Muth Labben."
A psalm of David.*

◆

2 With a heart full of thanks
　I proclaim your wonders, God.
3 You are my joy, my delight;
　I sing hymns to your name, Most High.
4 My foes retreated before you,
　they collapsed and died.

◆

5 You upheld my just cause,
　gave judgment from your throne.
6 You condemned the nations,
　destroyed the wicked,
　erased their names for ever.

7 You crushed my enemies,
　reduced them to ruins;
　their cities are rubble.
　Who remembers them?

◆

8 But you, God, reign for ever;
   you established your throne
9 to rule the world with justice
   and judge all peoples rightly.

10 You defend the oppressed,
    fortify them in time of trouble.
11 Those who know you, trust you;
    you never desert the faithful.

◆

12 Sing to the Lord of Zion,
    tell all people this wonder:
13 God avenges the poor
    and never neglects their cries.

◆

14 Pity me, Lord.
    How my enemies hurt me!
    From the gates of death you saved me,
15 so I might praise your deeds
    within the gates of Zion.
    I will rejoice in your victory.

◆

16 The nations fall into their own pit,
   caught by the traps they set.
17 The Lord shows power
   and wields judgment,
   traps the wicked in their own snares.

◆

18 They go down to Sheol.
   So much for the wicked,
   for nations that forget God!
19 The Lord never forgets the poor,
   never lets their hope die.

20 Rise up, O God,
   subdue the nations,
   judge them in your court.
21 Strike fear in them, Lord,
   let them know they are mortal. ☐

psalm 9

10

1 Where are you, Lord,
   when we need you?
   Why do you hide?

2 Sinners hound the poor
   with no remorse,
   but get tangled in
   their own schemes.

3 The wicked boast
   about their desires;
   greedy for profit,
   they curse the Lord.

4 They say with contempt,
   "God does not care!
   There is no God!"
5 They know their way to success;
   your ways are beyond them.
   They mock whoever resists them.

6 They claim to be invincible,
   beyond the reach of misfortune.
7 Their mouths breed
   curses, lies, and violence;

trouble and deceit
hide under their tongues.

8 They wait in ambush near towns;
from their hideouts
they watch for the helpless
and murder the innocent.

9 They lurk as a lion
waiting in a thicket
to carry off the poor.
They snare them in traps.

10 They crouch to the ground,
then pounce on their prey.
11 They think, "God forgets,
never looks, never sees."

12 Arise, God, and act;
do not ignore the weak.
13 Why do the wicked scorn you, God,
and think you do not care?

14 You observe our trouble and grief,
and at the right time
take things in hand.

The poor entrust their lives to you,
protector of orphans.
15 Break the strength of the brutal,
root out all traces of sin.

◆

16 You reign for ever, Lord,
keeping your land free
from foreign powers.

17 Lord, hear the longing of the poor,
listen to their every word,
and give them heart.
18 Then the orphaned and oppressed
will gain justice
and tyrants lose their power.   □

11

**THE LORD SEES ALL. GOD IS JUST
AND PROTECTS THOSE WHO DO JUSTICE.**

---

1 *For the choirmaster. Of David.*

◆

I have taken shelter in God,
so how can you say to me:
"Go, fly like a bird to the hills,
2 for the wicked bend their bows,
lock their arrows on the string

to shoot the just from the shadows.
3 When the world falls apart,
   what can the good hope to do?"

◆

4 God dwells in his holy temple,
   the heavens hold God's throne;
   the Lord watches the earth,
   eyes fixed on all nations,
5 weighing both righteous and wicked,
   rejecting the violent.
6 God sends a rain of fire,
   allots them a scorching wind.

7 The Lord loves justice,
   the just will see God's face.   □

12

*1 For the choirmaster. Upon the "eighth."
A psalm of David.*

◆

2 Help us, Lord,
for no one stays loyal,
the faithful have vanished.
3 People lie to each other,
no one speaks from the heart.

◆

4 May the Lord silence
the smooth tongue
and boasting lips that say:
5 "Our words will triumph!
With weapons like these
who can master us?"

◆

6 Then the Lord speaks out:
  "I will act now,
  for the poor are broken
  and the needy groan.
  When they call out,
  I will protect them."

◆

7 The Lord's word is pure,
  like silver from the furnace,
  seven times refined.

8 Lord, keep your promise,
  always protect your own.
  Guard them from this age
9 when wickedness abounds
  and evil is prized above all.   □

13

1 For the choirmaster. A psalm of David.

◆

2 Lord, will you ever remember me,
   why keep turning away from me?
3 Must I carry this grief for ever,
   how long endure this pain?
   Must my enemies always win?

◆

4 My God, look at me, answer me,
   shine on me or I will die;
5 never let my enemy boast,
   "See how you fall! I have won!"

6 I trust in your love
   and rejoice, for you save me;
7 I will sing to the Lord
   who treats me with kindness. □

14

---

1 *For the choirmaster. Of David.*

◆

Fools tell themselves,
"There is no God."
Their actions are corrupt,
none of them does good.

2 The Lord looks down
to see if anyone is wise,
if anyone seeks God.

3 But all have turned away,
all are depraved.
No one does good,
not even one.

◆

4 Are these evil-doers mad?
They eat up my people
like so much bread;
they never pray.

5 They should cringe in fear,
    for God sits with the just.
6 You may mock the poor,
    but the Lord keeps them safe.

◆

7 If only a savior would come from Zion
    to restore the people's fortunes!
    Then Jacob would sing,
    and Israel rejoice.   □

15

**IF YOU WOULD DWELL IN GOD'S PRESENCE,
ACT WITH INTEGRITY AND HONOR.**

1 *A psalm of David.*

◆

Lord, who is welcome in your house?
Who can rest on your holy mountain?

◆

2 Those who walk with integrity
and do only what is right,
speaking the truth with courage.

3 They never spread slander
or abuse their friends
or condemn their neighbors.

4 They disdain the godless,
but honor those who believe.
Before God, they give their word
and keep it at any cost.

5 They neither lend for gain
nor take bribes against the guiltless.
6 These are the just:
they stand for ever unshaken. □

16

---

1 A miktam of David.

◆

Protect me, God,
I turn to you for help.
2 I profess, "You are my Lord,
my greatest good."

3 I once put faith in false gods,
the idols of the land.
4 Now I make no offering to them,
nor invoke their names.
Those who chase after them
add grief upon grief.

5 Lord, you measure out my portion,
the shape of my future;
6 you mark off the best place for me
to enjoy my inheritance.

◆

7 I bless God who teaches me,
who schools my heart even at night.

8 I am sure God is here,
  right beside me.
  I cannot be shaken.

9 So my heart rejoices,
  my body thrills with life,
  my whole being rests secure.

10 You will not abandon me to Sheol,
   nor send your faithful one to death.
11 You show me the road to life:
   boundless joy at your side for ever! □

17

---

1 *A prayer of David.*

◆

Hear my just claim, God,
give me your full attention.
My prayer deserves an answer,
for I speak the truth.

2 Decide in my favor,
you always see what is right.

◆

3 You probed my heart,
tested me at night,
tried me by fire
but found nothing wrong.

Unlike others, I never lie.
4 I live your word, avoiding violence,
5 I walk your path and never stray.

◆

6 I call to you, God,
for you answer me.
Give me your attention,
hear me out.

7 Show me your wonderful love,
save the victims
of those who resist you.

8 Keep a loving eye on me.
Guard me under your wings,
9 hide me from those who attack,
from predators who surround me.
10 They close their heart,
they mouth contempt.

psalm 17

11 They stalk my path,
   ready to knock me down
12 like a lion hunting prey,
   waiting in ambush.

◆

13 Rise up, God,
   face them head on,
   draw your sword and slay them,
   save me from the wicked!
14 God, use your might
   and cut their lives short.

   But enrich those you love
   and give their children plenty
   to pass on to their young.
15 I will then be justified,
   will wake to see your face,
   and be filled with your presence. □

18

A PRAYER OF THANKSGIVING.
GOD IS FIRM FOUNDATION AND SURE DEFENSE.
GIVE PRAISE TO OUR STRENGTH AND SAVIOR.

---

1 For the choirmaster.
Of David, the servant of the Lord,
who addressed the words of this song
to the Lord after the Lord has rescued him
from the grasp of all his enemies
and from the hand of Saul. He said:

◆

2 I love you, God my strength,
3 my rock, my shelter, my stronghold.

My God, I lean on you,
my shield, my rock,
my champion, my defense.
4 When I call for help,
I am safe from my enemies.
Praise the Lord!

◆

5 Death had me in its grip,
the current swept me away;

6 Sheol was closing in,
   I felt the hand of death.

7 From the depths I cried out,
   my plea reached the heavens.
   God heard me.

◆

8 Then the earth shook:
   the mountains quaked,
   they rocked from side to side,
   trembled at God's anger.

9 With fiery breath and blazing nostrils
10 God split open the heavens,
    coming down on dense clouds,
11 riding on the cherubim throne,
    soaring aloft with the winds.

12 Cloaked in darkness,
    concealed in the rainstorm,
13 with flaming clouds,
    with hail and coals of fire,
14 the Lord almighty
    thundered from the heavens,
15 aimed lightning bolts like arrows
    to rout the enemy.

16 At your rebuke, Lord,
    when you bellowed in fury,
    the bed of the ocean,

psalm 18

the foundations of the earth,
were laid bare.
17 From on high God took hold of me,
lifted me clear of the deadly waters.

◆

18 My raging foes were strong,
stronger than I,
but God rescued me.
19 They rushed at me
on the day of disaster,
but the Lord upheld me.

20 God snatched me free,
led me to where I could breathe.
The Lord loved me.
21 I was just,
my hands were clean,
so the Lord rewarded me.

23 I have kept the commandments,
the laws set before me,
22 followed the path laid down,
never turned aside from my God.

24 I am without blame,
I have kept myself from evil.
25 The Lord gives me a just reward,
because my hands are clean.

26 To those who are faithful
you are faithful,

psalm 18

with those who are honest
you are candid.

27 To the just you show goodness,
with the perverse you are cunning.
28 You rescue the humble,
the mighty are brought low.

29 My God, you are my light,
a lamp for my darkness.
30 With strength from you, Lord,
I charge the enemy,
I climb their ramparts.

◆

31 God, your way is perfect,
your word is fire-tried.
You shield all who seek refuge.
32 Who is God but the Lord?
Who is the rock but our God?

33 Armed with your strength,
my way is sure.
34 You make me swift as a deer,
bounding over hills.
35 You train me for combat,
teach me to draw a mighty bow.

36 You gave me your shield for victory,
supported me with your right hand,
made me strong with your might.

37 I march out boldly,
my stride is firm.

38 I overtake my enemies,
not turning back
until they are no more.

39 I strike them down,
they lie dead at my feet.
40 You arm me for battle,
my enemies collapse.

41 I step on their necks
to destroy them.
42 They cry for help
but there is none,
they cry to the Lord,
but the Lord does not answer.

43 I grind them fine
as wind-blown dust,
toss them out
like rubbish in the streets.

44 You saved me from invaders,
made me ruler over nations.
Foreign people serve me.

45 They hear me and obey,
they cringe before me.
46 Exhausted and trembling,
they crawl out from hiding.

◆

47 The Lord lives!
   blessed be my rock,
   the God who saves me,
48 the God who avenges,
   who makes the nations submit.
49 You humble my foes,
   from the violent you rescue me.

50 Among the nations I praise you,
   sing your power and name.
51 You give great victory
   to your anointed king,
   you are faithful for all time
   to the house of David.   ☐

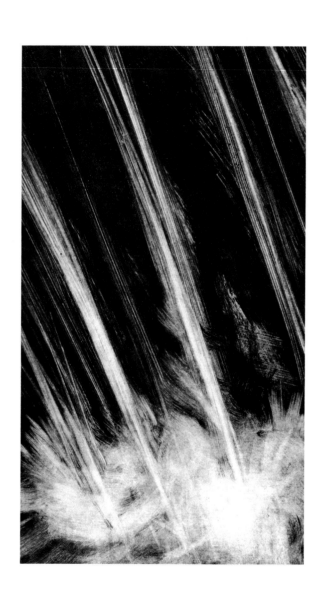

19

A MEDITATIVE HYMN.
THE LIGHTS OF THE SKY PROCLAIM GOD'S GLORY.
THE LIGHT OF GOD'S LAW ILLUMINES THE SPIRIT.

1 For the choirmaster. A psalm of David.

◆

2 The sky tells the glory of God,
  tells the genius of God's work.
3 Day carries the news to day,
  night brings the message to night,

4 without a word, without a sound,
  without a voice being heard,
5 yet their message fills the world,
  their news reaches its rim.

  There God has pitched a tent
  for the sun to rest and rise renewed
6 like a bridegroom rising from bed,
  an athlete eager to run the race.

7 It springs from the edge of the earth,
  runs a course across the sky
  to win the race at heaven's end.
  Nothing on earth escapes its heat.

◆

8 God's perfect law
revives the soul.
God's stable rule
guides the simple.

9 God's just demands
delight the heart.
God's clear commands
sharpen vision.

10 God's faultless decrees
stand for ever.
God's right judgments
keep their truth.

11 Their worth is more than gold,
the purest gold;
their taste richer than honey,
sweet from the comb.

12 Keeping them makes me rich,
they bring me light;
13 yet faults hide within us,
forgive me mine.

14 Keep my pride in check,
break its grip;
I shall be free of blame
for deadly sin.

15 Keep me, thought and word,
in your good grace.
Lord, you are my savior,
you are my rock.   □

20

**A PRAYER FOR THE RULER AT THE TIME OF WAR.
ISRAEL'S STRENGTH IS NOT MILITARY MIGHT.**

---

1 *For the choirmaster. A psalm of David.*

2 God defend you in battle!
set you safe above the fray!
3 The God of Jacob send you help,
and from holy Zion, keep you strong!

4 May God recall your many gifts
and be pleased with your sacrifice,
5 favoring all your hopes,
making your plans succeed.

6 Then we will sing of your conquest,
raise the flags in triumph,
to proclaim the name of our God
who grants all you ask.

◆

7 Now I know for certain:
the anointed of the Lord
is given victory.
God favors him from highest heaven
with a strong, saving hand.

8 Some boast of chariots and horses,
but we boast of God's name.
9 They waver and fall,
but we stand firm.

10 Lord, give victory to your king,
answer us on the day we call.   □

21

**GOD GIVES THE VICTORY TO THE ANOINTED ONE.
GOD IS SURE STRENGTH AND SAVING SHIELD.**

---

1 *For the choirmaster. A psalm of David.*

◆

2 Lord, the king triumphs with your help,
exults in the victory you gave;

3 you granted what he hoped for,
  accomplished what he asked.

4 You handed him this blessing
  and crowned him with gold;
5 he begged only to be spared,
  but you multiplied his years.

6 All his glory is in your victory,
  for you invest him with royal splendor,
7 confer on him lasting blessings,
  and give him joy in your presence.
8 The king relies on the Most High;
  God's love becomes his strength.

◆

9 Your hands search out your enemies,
  uncover all who hate you;
10 you burn them with your anger,
  consume them in your fiery blaze.
  Your fury swallows them,
  the fire devours them;
11 you purge them from the land
  and leave them no offspring.

12 For they plotted and schemed against you,
  but their evil did not succeed;
13 you made them turn and run
  from the deadly aim of your arrows.
14 Rejoice in your victory, Lord!
  We sing and praise your strength. □

22

---

1 *For the choirmaster to "The Hind of the Dawn."*
A psalm of David.

◆

2 God, my God,
 why have you abandoned me—
 far from my cry, my words of pain?
3 I call by day, you do not answer;
 I call by night, but find no rest.

4 You are the Holy One enthroned,
 the Praise of Israel.
5 Our people trusted, they trusted you;
 you rescued them.
6 To you they cried, and they were saved;
 they trusted and were not shamed.

7 But I am a worm, hardly human,
 despised by all, mocked by the crowd.
8 All who see me jeer at me,
 sneer at me, shaking their heads:
9 "You relied on God; let God help you!
 If God loves you, let God save you!"

10 But you, God, took me from the womb,
  you kept me safe at my mother's breast.
11 I belonged to you from the time of birth,
  you are my God from my mother's womb.

12 Do not stay far off,
  danger is so close.
  I have no other help.
13 Wild bulls surround me,
  bulls of Bashan encircle me,
14 opening their jaws against me
  like roaring, ravening lions.

15 I am poured out like water,
  my bones are pulled apart,
  my heart is wax melting within me,
16 my throat baked and dry,
  my tongue stuck to my jaws.
  You bring me down to the dust of death.

17 There are dogs all around me,
  a pack of villains corners me.
  They tear at my hands and feet,
18 I can count all my bones.
  They stare at me and gloat.
19 They take what I wore,
  they roll dice for my clothes.

20 Lord, do not stay far off,
  you, my strength, be quick to help.
21 Save my neck from the sword,
  save my life from the dog's teeth,

psalm 22

22 save me from the lion's jaws,
   save me from the bull's horns.

You hear me.

◆

23 I will proclaim your name to my people,
   I will praise you in the assembly.

24 Give praise, all who fear God:
   revere and honor the Lord,
   children of Israel, people of Jacob.
25 The Lord never scorns the afflicted,
   never looks away, but hears their cry.

26 I will sing of you in the great assembly,
   make good my promise before your faithful.
27 The poor shall eat all they want.
   Seekers of God shall give praise.
   "May your hearts live for ever!"

28 All peoples shall remember and turn,
   all races will bow to the Lord,
29 who holds dominion over nations.
30 The well-fed crowd kneel before God,
   all destined to die bow low.

31 My soul lives for the Lord!
   My children will serve,
   will proclaim God to the future,
32 announcing to peoples yet unborn,
   "God saves." □

23

1 A psalm of David.

◆

The Lord is my shepherd,
I need nothing more.
2 You give me rest in green meadows,
setting me near calm waters,
where you revive my spirit.

3 You guide me along sure paths,
you are true to your name.
4 Though I should walk
    in death's dark valley,
I fear no evil with you by my side,
your shepherd's staff to comfort me.

◆

5 You spread a table before me
as my foes look on.
You soothe my head with oil;
my cup is more than full.

6 Goodness and love will tend me
  every day of my life.
  I will dwell in the house of the Lord
  as long as I shall live. □

24

**A HYMN TO ACCLAIM GOD'S SOVEREIGNTY
OVER ALL CREATION.
WELCOME THE LORD!**

---

1 A psalm of David.

God owns this planet
and all its riches.
The earth and every creature
belong to God.

2 God set the land on top of the seas
  and anchored it in the deep.

3 Who is fit to climb God's mountain
  and stand in his holy place?

4 Whoever has integrity:
not chasing shadows,
not living lies.

5 God will bless them,
their savior will bring justice.
6 These people long to see the Lord,
they seek the face of Jacob's God.

◆

7 Stretch toward heaven, you gates,
open high and wide.
Let the glorious sovereign enter.

8 Who is this splendid ruler?
The Lord of power and might,
the conqueror of chaos.

9 Stretch toward heaven, you gates,
open high and wide.
Let the glorious sovereign enter.

10 Who is this splendid ruler?
The Lord of heaven's might,
this splendid ruler is God.   □

25

---

1 *Of David.*

◆

Lord, I give myself to you.

2 I trust you, God;
   do not fail me,
   nor let my enemies gloat.
3 No one loyal is shamed,
   but traitors know disgrace.

4 Teach me how to live,
   Lord, show me the way.
5 Steer me toward your truth,
   you, my saving God,
   you, my constant hope.

6 Recall your tenderness,
   your lasting love.
7 Remember me, not my faults,
   the sins of my youth.
   To show your own goodness,
   God, remember me.

◆

8 Good and just is the Lord,
  guiding those who stray.
9 God leads the poor,
  pointing out the path.

10 God's ways are faithful love
   for those who keep the covenant.
11 Be true to your name, O Lord,
   forgive my sin, though great.

12 Do you respect God?
   Then God will guide your choice.
13 Your life will be full,
   your heirs will keep the land.
14 God befriends the faithful,
   teaches them the covenant.

◆

15 I keep looking to God
   to spring me from this trap.
16 Turn, treat me as your friend,
   I am empty and poor.

17 Release my trapped heart,
   free me from my anguish.
18 See my misery, my pain,
   take my sins away.

19 See how they mob me,
   this crowd that hates me.

psalm 25

20 Protect me and save my life.
   Keep me from disgrace,
   for I take shelter in you.
21 Let integrity stand guard
   as I wait for you.

22 Free Israel, O God,
   from all its troubles. □

26

**WITH INTEGRITY AND CONFIDENCE,
SEEK GOD'S HELP.
RENDER YOUR THANKS AND PRAISE.**

---

1 Of David.

Lord, defend me!
I have walked with honesty,
I trusted the Lord without wavering.
2 Test me, try me, Lord,
   probe my heart and soul.

◆

3 Your love is ever before me,
   I walk boldly with your strength.
4 I do not sit with liars,
   I do not mix with hypocrites.
5 I hate evil company,
   I shall not live with crime.

6 I wash my hands in innocence
   and walk around your altar,
7 singing a song of thanks,
   telling your wonderful deeds.
8 Lord, I love your house,
   the place your glory rests.

◆

9 Class me not with sinners,
   my life with the violent,
10 those with criminal hands,
    hands filled with bribes.

11 Yes, I will be honest.
    Rescue me, be gracious!
12 My stance is firm.
    At gatherings, I bless the Lord.   □

psalm 26

27

1 Of David.

◆

The Lord is my saving light;
whom should I fear?
God is my fortress;
what should I dread?

2 When the violent come at me
to eat me alive,
a mob eager to kill—
they waver, they collapse.

3 Should battalions lay siege,
I will not fear;
should war rage against me,
even then I will trust.

4 One thing I ask the Lord,
one thing I seek:
to live in the house of God
every day of my life,
caught up in God's beauty,
at prayer in his temple.

5 The Lord will hide me there,
  hide my life from attack:
  a sheltering tent above me,
  a firm rock below.

6 I am now beyond reach
  of those who besiege me.
  In his temple I will offer
  a joyful sacrifice,
  I will play and sing to God.

◆

7 O God, listen to me;
  be gracious, answer me.
8 Deep within me a voice says,
  "Look for the face of God!"

  So I look for your face,
9 I beg you not to hide.
  Do not shut me out in anger,
  help me instead.

  Do not abandon or desert me,
  my savior, my God.
10 If my parents rejected me,
  still God would take me in.

11 Teach me how to live,
  lead me on the right road
  away from my enemies.
12 Do not leave me to their malice;

liars breathing violence
rise to swear against me.

13 I know I will see
how good God is
while I am still alive.
14 Trust in the Lord. Be strong.
Be brave. Trust in the Lord.   □

28

**A PRAYER FOR DELIVERANCE AND VINDICATION.
GOD IS SHIELD AND SHEPHERD AND SAVIOR.**

---

1 *Of David.*

I call out, Lord my rock.
Do not be deaf,
do not keep silent.
Without you I must die.

2 Hear my cry for mercy,
my call for help;
I stretch out my hands
toward your holy temple.

3 Do not drag me off like the wicked
   who speak peace to friends
   but have malice in their hearts.

4 Pay them in their own coin.
   What they do is evil;
   give them what they deserve.

5 The ways of the Lord
   mean nothing to them.
   May God destroy their world
   and never rebuild it!

◆

6 Blessed be the Lord
   who hears my cry.
7 God is the strong shield
   in whom my heart trusts.

   When help comes to me,
   joy fills my heart
   and I thank God in song.
8 Strength comes from the Lord,
   salvation for his anointed.

9 Save your chosen people.
   Bless and shepherd them
   and keep them for ever.   □

29

1 A psalm of David.

◆

Give the Lord glory, you spirits!
Give glory! Honor God's strength!
2 Honor the name of the Lord!
Bow when the Lord comes,
majestic and holy.

◆

3 God's voice thunders
above the massive seas;
4 powerful, splendid,
5 God shatters the cedars,
shatters the cedars of Lebanon,
6 makes Lebanon jump like a calf,
Sirion like a wild ox.

7 God's voice strikes fire,
8 makes the desert shudder,
Qadesh shudder in labor,
9 deer writhe in labor.
God strips the trees.

◆

All shout "Glory" in your temple, Lord.
10 For you rule the mighty waters,
you rule over all for ever.
11 Give strength to your people, Lord,
and bless your people with peace.   □

30

**A JOYFUL HYMN OF THANKSGIVING.
GOD HEALS US AND RESTORES US TO LIFE.**

1 *A psalm. A song at the dedication of the temple.
Of David.*

◆

2 I give you high praise,
for you, Lord, raised me up
above my gloating enemy.
3 Lord, how I begged you,
and you, God, healed me.
4 You pulled me from the pit,
brought me back from Sheol.

5 Celebrate, all you saints,
praise this awesome God,

6 whose anger passes quickly,
   whose mercy lasts a lifetime —
   as laughter fills a day
   after one brief night of tears.

◆

7 When all was going well,
   I thought I could never fall;
8 with God's powerful blessing,
   I would stand like a mountain!
   Then you hid your face;
   I shook with fear!

◆

9 I cried out, "Lord, Lord!"
   I begged, I pleaded:
10 "What good is my blood to you?
   Why push me down the pit?
   Can dead bones praise you,
   recount your unbroken love?
11 Listen to me, O God,
   turn and help me now."

◆

12 You changed my anguish
   into this joyful dance,
   pulled off my sackcloth,
   gave me bright new robes,

13 that my life might sing your glory,
   never silent in your praise.
   For ever I will thank you,
   O Lord my God.   □

31

**A PRAYER FOR DELIVERANCE.
IN TIMES OF AFFLICTION,
REMEMBER GOD'S FIDELITY IN THE PAST.**

1 *For the choirmaster. A psalm of David.*

2 Shelter me, Lord,
   save me from shame.
   Let there be justice:
   save me!

3 Help me! Listen!
   Be quick to the rescue!
   Be my fortress, my refuge.

4 You, my rock and fortress,
   prove your good name.
   Guide me, lead me,
5 free me from their trap.

You are my shelter;
6 I put myself in your hands,
knowing you will save me,
Lord God of truth.

7 You hate the slaves of idols,
but I trust in you.
8 I dance for joy at your constant love.

You saw me suffer,
you know my pain.
9 You let no enemy cage me,
but set my feet on open ground.

◆

10 Pity me, Lord,
I hurt all over;
my eyes are swollen,
my heart and body ache.

11 Grief consumes my life,
sighs fill my days;
guilt saps my strength,
my bones dissolve.

12 Enemies mock me,
make me the butt of jokes.
Neighbors scorn me,
strangers avoid me.
13 Forgotten like the dead,
I am a shattered jar.

14 I hear the crowd whisper,
   "Attack on every side!"
   as they scheme to take my life.

15 But I trust in you, Lord.
   I say, "You are my God,
16 my life is in your hands."
   Snatch me from the enemy,
   ruthless in their chase.

17 Look on me with love,
   save your servant.
18 I call on you;
   save me from shame!

   Shame the guilty,
   silence them with the grave.
19 Silence the lips that lie,
   that scorn the just.

◆

20 How rich your goodness
   to those who revere you!
   The whole world can see:
   whoever seeks your help
   finds how lavish you are.

21 You are shelter from gossips,
   a place to hide from busy tongues.
22 Blessed be the Lord!
   God's love encircles me
   like a protecting wall.

psalm 31

23 I said too quickly,
   "God has cut me off!"
   But you heard my cry
   when I prayed for help.

24 Love the Lord, all faithful people,
   the Lord your guardian,
   who fully repays the proud.
25 Be strong, be brave,
   all who wait for God.   □

32

**A JOYOUS HYMN OF THANKSGIVING
FOR GOD'S FORGIVENESS.
SIN CONCEALED IS A BURDEN OF MISERY;
SIN CONFESSED FREES FROM HARM.**

1 *Of David. A maskil.*

◆

2 Happy the pardoned,
   whose sin is canceled,
   in whom God finds
   no evil, no deceit.

3 While I hid my sin,
  my bones grew weak
  from endless groaning.

4 Day and night,
  under the weight of your hand,
  my strength withered
  as in a summer drought.

5 Then I stopped hiding my sin
  and spoke out,
  "God, I confess my wrong."
  And you pardoned me.

6 No wonder the faithful
  pray to you in danger!
  Even a sudden flood
  will never touch them.

7 You, my shelter,
  you save me from ruin.
  You encircle me
  with songs of freedom.

◆

8 "I show you the path to walk.
  As your teacher,
  I watch out for you.

9 "Do not be a stubborn mule,
  needing bridle and bit
  to be tamed."

10 Evil brings grief;
   trusting in God brings love.

◆

Rejoice in the Lord.
Be glad and sing,
you faithful and just.   □

33

1 Shout joy to the Lord,
   lovers of justice,
   how right to praise!
2 Praise God on the harp,
   with ten-string lyre
   sing to the Lord.

3 Sing God a new song.
   Play music to match
   your shout of joy.

◆

4 For the word of the Lord is true:
   what God says, God does.
5 This lover of truth and justice
   fills the earth with love.

6 God speaks: the heavens are made;
   God breathes: the stars shine.
7 God bottles the waters of the sea
   and stores them in the deep.

8 All earth, be astounded,
   stand in awe of God.
9 God speaks: the world is;
   God commands: all things appear.

10 God blocks the plans of nations,
   disrupts all they contrive.
11 But God's plan and designs
   last from age to age.
12 Blest the land whose god is the Lord,
   the heirs whom God has chosen.

13 The Lord looks down
   and sees our human kind.
14 From heaven God surveys
   all peoples on earth.
15 The maker of human hearts
   knows every human act.

16 Armies do not save kings,
   brute force does not spare soldiers.

17 The warhorse is a sham;
   despite its power, it will not save.

18 God keeps a loving eye
   on all who believe,
   on those who count on God
19 to bring relief from famine,
   to rescue them from death.

◆

20 With all we are, we wait for God,
   the Lord, our help, our shield.
21 Our hearts find joy in the Lord;
   we trust God's holy name.
22 Love us, Lord!
   We wait for you. □

34

1 Of David,
when he pretended to be mad before Abimelek
so that he drove him out
and he went on his way.

◆

2 I will never stop thanking God,
   with constant words of praise.
3 My soul will boast of God;
   the poor will hear me and be glad.

4 Join me in praising the Lord,
   together tell of God's name.
5 I asked and the Lord responded,
   freed me from all my fears.

◆

6 Turn to God, be bright with joy;
   you shall never be let down.
7 I begged and God heard,
   took my burdens from me.

8 God's angel defends the faithful,
   guards them on every side.
9 Drink in the richness of God,
   enjoy the strength of the Lord.

10 Live in awe of God, you saints:
   you will want for nothing.
11 Even if lions go hungry,
   those seeking God are fed.

◆

12 Come to me, children, listen:
   learn to cherish the Lord.
13 Do you long for life,
   for time to enjoy success?

14 Keep your tongue from evil,
   keep lies far from your lips.
15 Shun evil, go after good,
   press on, seek after peace.

17 God confronts the wicked
   to blot them out for ever,
16 but turns toward the just
   to hear their cry for help.

18 The troubled call out; God hears,
   saves them from all distress.
19 God stays near broken hearts,
   heals the wounded spirit.

20 The good endure great trials,
   but God comes to their rescue

21 and guards their every bone
so not one is broken.

22 Evil kills its own kind,
dooms the wicked to death.
23 God saves those who keep faith;
no trusting soul is doomed. □

35

A DESPERATE PLEA FOR DELIVERANCE
FROM THOSE WHO BETRAY THEIR FRIENDS
AND REJOICE IN THE MISFORTUNES OF OTHERS.

1 *Of David.*

Lord, accuse my accusers,
battle those who battle me.
2 Take up shield and buckler
and rise to my defense.

3 Ready your axe and spear
to cut down my enemies.
Tell me you will save me.

4 Punish those who want me dead,
   make them retreat in disgrace,
   since they seek my life.

5 Let God's angel chase them
   as the wind drives the chaff.
6 Let God's angel pursue them
   down dark and slippery paths.

7 Without cause they dug a pit,
   for no good reason
   set a trap for me.

8 Catch them off guard,
   snare them in their own trap.
   Let them fall to their ruin.

9 Then I will rejoice in the Lord
   and celebrate God's victory.
10 From the marrow of my bones
   I will say: "Lord, who is like you,
   rescuing the weak from the strong,
   the victim from the robber."

◆

11 Witnesses come forward,
   they accuse me falsely
   of things I do not know.
12 They repay me evil for good,
   leaving me desolate.

13 When they were ill,
   I wore sackcloth and fasted,
   now I take back my prayer!

14 I mourned for them
   as for my brother or friend;
   I was weighed down with grief
   as if I had lost my mother.

15 But when I stumbled, they cheered;
   they gathered to tear at me
   and I did not know why.
   They would not stop their attack.
16 The godless taunted me,
   they clenched their teeth and mocked.

17 Lord, how long will you look on?
   Save me from these roaring lions,
   my life is precious.
18 Then I will thank you
   when the assembly gathers
   and praise you before the crowd.

◆

19 Give my lying enemies
   no chance to gloat,
   my reckless foes
   no chance to smirk.

psalm 35

20 They do not speak peace
but devise schemes
to disrupt the land.
21 They laugh openly at me,
"See what happened to you!"

22 Lord, you see it all!
Do not keep silent,
do not stand aloof.
23 Wake, rouse yourself in my defense.
Take up my cause, my Lord and God.

24 As you are just,
judge in my favor.
Do not give them the last word.
25 Do not let them think,
"Yes, we got our way."
Do not let them say,
"We finished you off."

26 When they delight in my ruin,
bring them disgrace.
When they gloat at my expense,
cover them with shame.

27 But let my friends rejoice
when they see me avenged.
Let them shout and say always,
"Great is the God who is pleased
when a faithful servant triumphs."

28 Then I will tell of your justice,
sing your praises all day long. □

36

*1 For the choirmaster.
Of David, the servant of the Lord.*

◆

2 Sin whispers with the wicked,
  shares its evil, heart to heart.
  These sinners shut their eyes
  to all fear of God.
3 They refuse to see their sin,
  to know it and hate it.

4 Their words ring false and empty,
  their plans neglect what is good.
5 They daydream of evil,
  plot their crooked ways,
  seizing on all that is vile.

◆

6 Your mercy, Lord, spans the sky;
  your faithfulness soars among the clouds.
7 Your integrity towers like a mountain;
  your justice runs deeper than the sea.

Lord, you embrace all life:
8 How we prize your tender mercy!

God, your people seek shelter,
safe in the warmth of your wings.
9 They feast at your full table,
slake their thirst in your cool stream,
10 for you are the fount of life,
you give us light and we see.

◆

11 Grant mercy always to your own,
victory to honest hearts.
12 Keep the proud from trampling me,
assaulting me with wicked hands.
13 Let those sinners collapse,
struck down, never to rise. □

37

1 Of David.

No need to fret over sinners
or to envy wrongdoers.
2 They wither like grass,
they wilt like young plants.

3 Trust God and do good,
settle down and be at peace.
4 Delight in the Lord
who satisfies your heart.

5 Give your life to the Lord.
Trust God to act on your behalf,
6 to make your integrity shine forth
and your justice bright as noon.

7 Be still, wait for the Lord.
Waste no energy fretting
about the success of evil schemers.
8 Stop your ranting and raving,
for anger begets nothing but harm.

9 Wrongdoers will be exiled,
but those who wait for God
will possess the land.
10 Soon the wicked shall vanish,

you will search and not find them;
11 but the poor will own the land
and enjoy wealth and peace.

12 The wicked bare their teeth in rage
as they plot against the just.
13 But God laughs at them,
knowing their end is near.

14 The wicked draw the sword
and string the bow
to kill the weak and helpless,
to murder the law-abiding.

15 But they will fall on their swords,
their bows will be broken.
16 Better to have little and be just,
than to own much and do evil.

17 The strength of the wicked will be crushed,
but God will support the just.
18 Each day the Lord protects
the lives of the blameless;
their inheritance endures.

19 In bad times they are not shamed,
in famine they eat their fill.
20 The enemies of God will die;
they go up in smoke,
burn like summer grass.

21 The wicked take but never repay,
the just give without complaint.

22 The blest inherit the land,
   but the cursed are cut off.

23 God steadies the faithful
   and is pleased with their ways.
24 If they stumble they do not fall,
   for God holds their hands.

25 From my youth to my old age
   never have I seen the just cast off
   or their children begging bread.
26 Goodness and giving fill their days;
   their offspring become a blessing.

27 Turn from evil and do good
   and you will live for ever.
28 For the Lord loves justice
   and never deserts the faithful.
   But the wicked will perish
   and their children will die.

29 The just will gain the land
   and hold it for ever.
30 They have wisdom on their tongues
   and justice on their lips.
31 With God's teaching in their hearts,
   they do not falter.

32 The wicked track the faithful,
   hoping to condemn them.
33 But God never abandons the just,
   nor permits a verdict against them.

34 Wait in hope and keep God's way,
   the Lord will give you power.
   You will have your land
   and watch the wicked fall.

35 I have seen the wicked flourish
   like a deeply rooted tree.
36 I came by and they had vanished;
   I searched but they were gone.

37 Observe the honest and upright:
   the future belongs to peacemakers.
38 But the violent will be destroyed;
   there is no future for the wicked.

39 The just are saved by God,
   their refuge in troubled times.
40 They seek help from God
   who saves and rescues them,
   who saves and frees them
      from the wicked.   □

38

1 A psalm of David. For remembrance.

◆

2 God, do not punish me
or strike me in your anger.
3 Your arrows have pierced deep,
your hand has struck hard.

4 Because of your wrath,
my whole body withers.
Because of my sin,
all my bones grow brittle.

5 For my sins weigh me down,
too heavy to bear.
6 My wounds fester and reek
because of my folly.

◆

7 Bent over and humbled,
I walk in misery all day long.
8 Fever consumes me;
there is no health in my body.

9 Feeble and broken, I cry out,
  groaning from the heart.

10 Lord, you see what I long for,
   you hear all my sighs.
11 My heart pounds, my strength fails,
   the light of my eyes is snuffed out.

12 Friends and neighbors avoid me,
   keeping their distance.
13 My mortal foes scheme against me,
   hatching plots day after day
   and spreading lies to trap me.

◆

14 Like someone born deaf
   or unable to speak,
15 I can no longer hear,
   I have no words for my defense.
16 But I wait for you, Lord,
   and you, my God, will answer.

17 I said, "Don't let them gloat,
   those who laugh when I fall."
18 For I am about to collapse,
   there is no relief from my pain.

◆

19 I know my guilt
   and grieve over my sin.
20 My enemies are strong;

many hate me for no reason.
21 Those who deal evil for good
blame me for seeking what is right.

22 Do not abandon me, God,
do not stay far from me.
23 Hurry, Lord, help me!
for you keep me safe. □

39

**A CRY FOR HELP IN THE FACE OF TORMENT.
GOD ALONE CAN GRANT REPRIEVE.**

---

1 *For the choirmaster. For Jeduthun.
A psalm of David.*

2 I said I will not sin!
I will curb my tongue
and muzzle my mouth
when the wicked confront me.

3 I kept silent,
would not say a word,
yet my anguish grew.
4 It scorched my heart

and seared my thoughts
until I had to speak.

◆

5 Lord, what will become of me?
How long will I live?
Let me see how short life is!

6 You give me a brief span of time;
before you, my days are nothing.
People are but a breath:
7 they walk like shadows;
their efforts amount to nothing;
they hoard, but others gain.

◆

8 Why do I wait for you, Lord?
You are my hope
9 to save me from my sins;
do not make a fool of me.
10 I will keep quiet.
I have said enough,
since all this is your doing.

11 Stop tormenting me;
you strike and I grow weak.
12 You rebuke us for our sin,
eat up our riches like a moth;
we are but a breath.

13 Lord, hear my prayer,
   my cry for help.
   Do not ignore my tears,
   as if I were alien to you,
   a stranger like my ancestors.
14 Stop looking so hard at me,
   allow me a little joy
   before I am no more.   □

40

**THANKSGIVING FOR DELIVERANCE
AND PRAYER FOR GOD'S CONTINUED PROTECTION.
IN AFFLICTION AND SADNESS, RELY ON GOD.**

1 For the choirmaster. A psalm of David.

◆

2 I waited and waited for God.
   At long last God bent down
   to hear my complaint,
3 and pulled me from the grave
   out of the swamp,
   and gave me a steady stride
   on rock-solid ground.

4 God taught me a new song,
   a hymn of praise.
   Seeing all this,
   many will be moved
   to trust in the Lord.

5 Happy are they who trust in God,
   not seduced by idols
   nor won over by lies.

6 You do so many wonders,
   you show you care for us,
   Lord my God;
   you are beyond compare.
   Were I to name them all,
   no one could keep track.

7 You did not seek offerings
   or ask for sacrifices;
   but you drilled ears
   for me to hear.

8 "Yes," I said, "I will come
   to live by your written word."
9 I want to do what pleases you;
   your teaching is in my heart.

10 I celebrate your justice
   before all the assembly;
   I do not hold back the story.
   Lord, you know this is true.

11 I did not hide in my heart
   your acts of rescue;

I boldly declared to all
your truth and care, your faithful love.

12 Your maternal love
surrounds me, Lord.
Your sure and tender care
protects me always.

◆

13 Countless evils surround me,
more than the hairs on my head;
my sins overwhelm me,
so many I can hardly see.
My courage fails me.

14 Please, Lord, rescue me;
hurry, Lord, help me.
15 Stop my killers, shame them,
wipe out my bitter enemies.

16 Let those who jeer at me,
"Too bad for you!"
be rewarded with shame.

17 But let all who seek you
and count on your strength
sing and dance and cheer
"Glory to God!"

18 Though I am weak and poor,
God cares for me.
My help, my savior,
my God, act now!   □

psalm 40

41

1 For the choirmaster. A psalm of David.

2 Blest are those ready to help the poor;
in hard times God repays their care.

3 God watches, protects,
blesses them in their land,
lets no enemy swallow them up!
4 God comforts them on their sickbed
and nurses them to health.

5 I said, "God, pity me,
heal me for I have failed you."
6 Enemies predict the worst for me:
"How soon till this one dies,
how soon forgotten?"

7 Visitors all wish me well,
but they come seeking bad news
to gossip on the street.

8 My enemies whisper
and spread the worst about me:
9 "Something fatal has taken hold,
this one will not get well."

10 Even my trusted friend
who used to eat with me
now turns on me.

11 Pity me, God, restore me
so I can pay them back.
12 Then I will know you favor me
when my foes cannot prevail.
13 I am innocent; uphold me!
Let me stand with you for ever.

14 Blessed be the Lord,
God of Israel for ever.
Amen! Amen! □

42

*1 For the choirmaster.
A maskil of the sons of Korah.*

◆

2 As a deer craves running water,
   I thirst for you, my God;
3 I thirst for God,
   the living God.
   When will I see your face?

4 Tears are my steady diet.
   Day and night I hear,
   "Where is your God?"

5 I cry my heart out,
   I remember better days:
   when I entered the house of God,
   I was caught in the joyful sound
   of pilgrims giving thanks.

6 Why are you sad, my heart?
   Why do you grieve?
   Wait for the Lord.
   I will yet praise God my savior.

◆

7 My heart is sad.
  Even from Jordan and Hermon,
  from the peak of Mizar,
  I remember you.

8 There the deep roars to deep;
  your torrents crash over me.
9 The love God summoned by day
  sustained my praise by night,
  my prayer to the living God.

10 I complain to God,
   who I thought was rock:
   "Why have you forgotten me?
   Why am I bent double
   under the weight of enemies?

11 "Their insults grind me to dust.
   Day and night they say,
   'Where is your God?'"

12 Why are you sad, my heart?
   Why do you grieve?
   Wait for the Lord.
   I will yet praise God my savior. □

43

1 Decide in my favor, God,
  plead my case against the hateful,
  defend me from liars and thugs.
2 For you are God my fortress.

  Why have you forgotten me?
  Why am I bent double
  under the weight of enemies?

3 Send your light and truth.
  They will escort me
  to the holy mountain
  where you make your home.

4 I will approach the altar of God,
  God, my highest joy,
  and praise you with the harp,
  God, my God.

5 Why are you sad, my heart?
  Why do you grieve?
  Wait for the Lord.
  I will yet praise God my savior. □

44

---

*1 For the choirmaster.
A maskil of the sons of Korah.*

◆

2 We have heard the story
  our ancestors told us
  of your deeds so long ago:
3 how you, God, uprooted nations
  to plant your own people,
  how you weeded out others
  so they could flourish.

4 Sword did not win the land,
  might did not bring the victory;
  it was your power, your light,
  your love for them.

5 You, my God and King,
  led Jacob to victory.
6 By the power of your name
  we defeated our enemies,
  crushing those who rose against us.

7 I did not rely on my bow,
  my sword did not save me.
8 You, God, rescued us from danger
  and put our foes to shame.
9 Every day we praise your name,
  we never fail to thank you.

10 Yet you scorn and demean us,
  no longer march at our side.
11 You force us to retreat
  while the enemy plunders our goods.

12 You make us sheep for the slaughter,
  scatter us among the nations.
13 You sell us for a pittance
  and gain nothing in the bargain.

14 You reproach us before our neighbors;
  they scoff and sneer,
15 making a joke of us,
  shaking their heads.

16 Disgrace confronts me all day,
  I turn red with shame
17 when I hear cruel taunts
  from foes wanting revenge.

18 We endured all this,
  though we did not forget you

or betray your covenant.
19 We have not turned from you
   or wavered from your path.
20 Yet you banished us to the wilderness
   where darkness overwhelms us.

21 If we should forget your name
   and raise a prayer to foreign gods,
22 would you not find it out?
   You know the secrets of the heart.
23 Still we are killed for your sake,
   treated like sheep for slaughter.

◆

24 Wake up! Why do you sleep, Lord?
   Wake up! Do not reject us for ever!
25 Why do you hide from us?
   Why ignore how much we suffer?

26 We grovel in the dust,
   clutching at the ground.
27 Wake up and help us.
   Rescue us! Your love demands it.   □

45

**A HYMN FOR THE ROYAL WEDDING.
BLESS THE LORD IN FESTIVITY AND BEAUTY,
IN FIDELITY TO THE COVENANT,
IN THE JOY OF HUMAN LOVE.**

*1 For the choirmaster.
According to "The Lilies."
A maskil of the sons of Korah.
A love song.*

◆

2 A great song fills my heart,
   I will recite it to the king,
   my tongue as skilled as the scribal pen.

◆

For the king

3 Unrivaled in beauty,
   gracious in speech—
   how God has blessed you!

4 Hero, take up your sword,
   majestic in your armor.
5 Ride on for truth,
   show justice to the poor,
   wield your power boldly.

6 Your weapons are ready;
  nations fall beneath your might,
  your enemies lose heart.

7 Your throne is as lasting
  as the everlasting God.
  Integrity is the law of your land.

8 Because you love justice and hate evil,
  God, your God, anoints you
  above your peers with festive oil.

9 Your clothes are fragrant
  with myrrh and aloes
  and cinnamon flowers.
  Music of strings welcomes you
  to the ivory palace
  and lifts your heart.

10 Royal women honor you.
   On your right hand the queen,
   wearing gold of Ophir.

◆

For the queen

11 Mark these words, daughter:
   leave your family behind,
   forget your father's house.

12 The king desires your beauty.
   He is your lord.

13 Tyre comes with gifts,
the wealthy honor you.

14 The robes of the queen
are embroidered with gold.
15 In brilliant attire
she is led to the king;
her attendants follow.
16 In high spirits
they enter the royal palace.

◆

For the king

17 Your sons will inherit
the throne your fathers held.
They shall reign throughout the land.

18 Every age will recall your name.
This song will fix it in their memory. ☐

46

NEITHER NATURAL DISASTER NOR MILITARY FORCE
WILL MATTER BEFORE THE POWER OF GOD.
REST SECURE IN GOD'S PROTECTION.

*1 For the choirmaster.
A song of the sons of Korah.
According to "Virgins."*

◆

2 Our sure defense,
  our shelter and help in trouble,
  God never stands far off.

3 So we stand unshaken
  when solid earth cracks
  and volcanoes slide into the sea,
4 when breakers rage
  and mountains tremble in the swell.

  The Lord of cosmic power,
  Jacob's God, will shield us.

◆

5 A river delights the city of God,
  home of the Holy One Most High.
6 With God there, the city stands;
  God defends it under attack.

7 Nations rage, empires fall.
  God speaks, earth melts.

8 The Lord of cosmic power,
  Jacob's God, will shield us.

◆

9 Come! See the wonders
  God does across the earth:
10 everywhere stopping wars,
  smashing, crushing, burning
  all the weapons of war.

11 An end to your fighting!
  Acknowledge me as God,
  high over nations, high over earth.

12 The Lord of cosmic power,
  Jacob's God, will shield us. □

psalm 46

47

1 *For the choirmaster.*
A psalm of the sons of Korah.

◆

2 All peoples, clap your hands,
   shout your joy to God.
3 For God Most High is awesome,
   great king of all the earth.

4 The One who conquers peoples
   and sets them at our feet
5 chooses for beloved Jacob
   a land to be our pride.

◆

6 God ascends the mountain
   to cheers and trumpet blasts.
7 Sing out your praise to God,
   to the king, sing out your praise.

◆

8 For God rules the earth;
   sing praise with all your skill.
9 God rules over nations,
   high on the sacred throne.

10 Foreign rulers join
   the people of Abraham's God;
   all the powers on earth
   belong to God on high. □

48

**A SONG FOR JERUSALEM, THE CITY OF GOD.
FIRM IN FOUNDATION, SURE IN DEFENSE,
REVEL IN GOD'S CONSTANT LOVE.**

---

1 A song. A psalm of the sons of Korah.

◆

Our great Lord
deserves great praise
in the city of God:

2 Holy mountain, beautiful height,
   crown of the earth!

3 Zion, highest of sacred peaks,
   city of the Great King!
4 God enthroned in its palaces
   becomes our sure defense!

◆

5 Watch the foreign kings
   massing to attack;
6 seeing what they face,
   they flee in terror.

7 Trembling grips them,
   anguish like childbirth,
8 fury like an east wind
   shattering a merchant fleet.

◆

9 What we see
   matches what we were told,
   "This is the city the Lord protects;
   our God is strong for ever."
10 In your temple, Lord,
   we recall your constant love.

11 Your praise, like your name,
   fills the whole world.
   Your right hand holds the victory.
12 Mount Zion and the cities of Judah
   rejoice at your justice.

◆

13 March around Zion,
make the circuit,
count each tower.
Ponder these walls,
observe these citadels,

15 so you may tell your children:
"Here is God!
Our God for ever!
God who leads us
even against death!"

49

**WEALTH IS FLEETING; MORTALS PERISH.
TRUE RICHES ARE FOUND ONLY IN GOD.**

———

1 *For the choirmaster.
A psalm of the sons of Korah.*

◆

2 Everyone, take heed,
all the world, listen,

3 high and low,
  rich and poor alike.

4 I have wisdom you need to hear.
  I see to the heart of things.
5 I tune my ear to the truth
  and set my insight to music.

◆

6 Why should I be afraid in bad times
  when enemies surround me,
7 disdainful in their power,
  arrogant in their wealth?

8 We cannot save ourselves,
  cannot set things right with God;
9 the price is too high,
  well beyond our means.

10 There is no escaping death,
   no avoiding the grave.
11 Look, even the wisest die.
   Fools and idiots perish with them,
   and others claim their wealth.

12 The grave is the only home
   where they settle for good,
   even if their land
   still bears their name.

13 No matter how great,
   no one sees the truth:
   we die like beasts.

◆

14 Here is the fate of those
   only concerned for themselves:
15 they go straight to Sheol.

   Death shepherds them
   right into the grave,
   where flesh is eaten up
   and earth consumes them.

16 But I know God will rescue me,
   save me from the grip of death.

◆

17 Do not worry about wealth,
   when someone else becomes rich.
18 You cannot take it to your grave,
   wealth is worth nothing in death.

19 No matter how wealthy,
   no matter how many tell you,
   "My, how well you have done,"
20 the rich all join the dead
   never to see light again.

21 No matter how great,
   no one sees the truth:
   we die like beasts. □

psalm 49

50

GOD SUMMONS THE EARTH TO JUDGMENT:
RENDER YOUR ACCOUNT.
MAKE GOOD YOUR PROMISES.

---

1 A psalm of Asaph.

◆

The Lord, greater than all gods,
summons the earth from east to west,
2 makes light shine from Zion,
beauty beyond compare.

3 The Lord will not be silent
but comes in fire and storm
4 to summon earth and heaven
as witness to our trial:

5 "Gather the faithful
who seal my covenant with sacrifice."
6 The heavens will testify
that God, our judge, is just.

◆

7 "Listen, my people,
hear what I say.
I, your judge,

indict you, Israel.
I, your God.

8 "Despite your offerings,
despite your daily gifts,
I bring charges against you.
9 I have no need for
oxen from your stalls
or goats from your pens.

10 "I own all the forest beasts,
the cattle on a thousand hills.
11 I know all the mountain birds,
every creature of the field.
12 Hungry, I would not come to you,
I own the world and its riches.

13 "Do I eat the meat of bulls
and drink the blood of goats?
14 Instead of sacrifice, give thanks,
keep your promises to God.

15 "When in trouble, call out to me;
when I save you, sing my praise."

16 God tells the evildoer:
"How dare you quote my law to me
and invoke the covenant?
17 You hate my guidance,
you turn your back when I speak.

18 "Meet a thief
and you are instant friends.
You are at home with adultery.

19 "Your mouth serves evil,
and your tongue savors deceit.
20 You malign your family
and slander your own kin.
21 This is how you act.

"If I kept silent
you would think I am like you.
So I will indict you
and bring my case against you.

22 "Think hard about these things,
you who ignore God,
for if I rip you apart
you have no one to save you.

23 "Who thanks me, honors me.
Who keeps my way, I save." □

51

A PRAYER OF REPENTANCE.
THE SINNER PLEAS TO THE TENDER GOD
TO BE MADE WHOLE, TO BE A NEW CREATION.

———

1 *For the choirmaster. A psalm of David,*
2 *when Nathan the prophet came to him,*
   after he had gone to Bathsheba.

◆

3 Have mercy, tender God,
   forget that I defied you.
4 Wash away my sin,
   cleanse me from my guilt.

◆

5 I know my evil well,
   it stares me in the face,
6 evil done to you alone
   before your very eyes.

   How right your condemnation!
   Your verdict clearly just.
7 You see me for what I am,
   a sinner before my birth.

8 You love those centered in truth;
   teach me your hidden wisdom.
9 Wash me with fresh water,
   wash me bright as snow.

10 Fill me with happy songs,
   let the bones you bruised now dance.
11 Shut your eyes to my sin,
   make my guilt disappear.

12 Creator, reshape my heart,
   God, steady my spirit.
13 Do not cast me aside
   stripped of your holy spirit.

14 Save me, bring back my joy,
   support me, strengthen my will.
15 Then I will teach your way
   and sinners will turn to you.

16 Help me, stop my tears,
   and I will sing your goodness.
17 Lord, give me words
   and I will shout your praise.

18 When I offer a holocaust,
   the gift does not please you.
19 So I offer my shattered spirit;
   a changed heart you welcome.

psalm 51

◆

20 In your love make Zion lovely,
   rebuild the walls of Jerusalem.
21 Then sacrifice will please you,
   young bulls upon your altar.   □

52

STUBBORN FAITH IN GOD'S JUSTICE.
NOTHING CAN SHIELD THE MALICIOUS.
NO SLASHING WORDS CAN DESTROY
THOSE WHO TRUST IN GOD.

1 *For the choirmaster. A maskil of David,*
2 *when Doeg the Edomite came and told Saul,*
   "David has gone to Abimelech's house."

◆

3 Proud sinner, why do you brag?
   Why trumpet your crimes,
   your sins against the faithful?
4 Each day you plot their ruin,
   slash them with a razor tongue.

5 You prize evil over good,
   deceit over truthful speech.

6 O tongue full of lies,
   you love the word that hurts!

◆

7 But God will demolish you,
   snatch you away for ever,
   sweep you from your tent,
   uproot you from the living earth.

◆

8 The faithful watch in awe,
   then laugh with disdain:
9 "God was not your stronghold;
   you trusted in your wealth,
   found strength in your crimes."

10 But I am like an olive tree
   growing in the temple court,
   I trust God's love for ever.

11 I always give you thanks
   for what you, my God, have done.
   I proclaim your good name
   before your faithful people. □

53

*1 For the choirmaster.
According to "Mahalath."
A maskil of David.*

2 Fools tell themselves,
   "There is no God."
   Their actions are corrupt,
   none of them does good.

3 The Lord looks down
   to see if anyone is wise,
   if anyone seeks God.

4 But all are worthless,
   all are depraved.
   No one does good,
   not even one.

◆

5 Are these evil-doers mad?
   They eat up my people
   like so much bread;
   they never pray.

6 They should cringe in fear
   as never before,
   since God will scatter their bones.
   Your attackers may shame you,
   but God rejects them.

◆

7 Let God send victory from Zion
   and restore the people's fortunes!
   Then Jacob will sing,
   and Israel rejoice.   □

54

A DESPERATE PLEA FOR RESCUE.
GOD IS FAITHFUL.

---

*1 For the choirmaster.
For stringed instruments. A maskil of David,
2 when the Ziphites came and told Saul,
"Know that David is hiding among us."*

◆

3 Judge in my favor, Lord,
　use your power to save me.
4 O God, hear this plea,
　listen to what I say.

5 For godless people attack me,
　strangers without conscience
　plotting my death.

◆

6 But God is my savior,
　God alone guards my life.

7 Let their evil rebound
　on all who plot against me.
　True to your judgment, Lord,
　put an end to them.

8 With a free heart
   I will sacrifice to you
   and praise your good name.
9 You saved me from danger,
   I see my enemies routed.   □

55

**CITIES ARE FULL OF VIOLENCE.
EVEN FRIENDS CANNOT BE TRUSTED: ONLY GOD.**

1 *For the choirmaster. For stringed instruments.
   A maskil of David.*

2 Listen, God, to my plea,
   do not ignore my cry.
3 Listen and answer,
   I shake with grief
4 at the furor of my enemies.
   They threaten and attack me;
   they shout out curses,
   venting their anger against me.

5 My heart is pounding,
   I can feel the touch of death.
6 Terror holds me in its grip,
   trembling seizes me.

7 "If I had wings like a dove,
   I would fly far and rest,
8 fly far away to the wilds
9 to escape the raging storm."

10 Confuse their speech, Lord!
   I see violence and strife
11 stalk their city walls
   both day and night.

   Evil and destruction
   live in their midst;
12 oppression and deceit
   never leave the public square.

13 If my enemy insults me,
   I can bear it;
   if a foe rises against me,
   I can hide myself.

14 But it was you, my own friend,
   the one I knew so well.
15 With you I could always talk,
   even as we walked to the temple,
   my companion amid the crowd.

◆

16 Death to them all!
   Let them fall into Sheol alive,
   for evil fills their homes
   and lives among them.

17 I call out to God
   who rescues me.
18 Morning, noon, and night
   I plead my case.

19 God hears my cry,
   brings me to safety
   when the battle is raging
   and my foes are many.

20 Enthroned for ever,
   God acts by humbling them
   because they refuse to change;
   they will not fear God.

21 My friend turned traitor
   and broke old promises,
22 spoke words smooth as butter
   while intending war,
   words that flowed like oil
   but cut like a sword.

23 Give your burden to the Lord,
   who will be your support.
   If you are faithful,
   God will not let you fall.

◆

24 O God, hurl the bloodthirsty
   into the pit of destruction.
   Let traitors live only half their days.
   But as for me, I trust in you. □

psalm 55

56

1 For the choirmaster.
According to "The Dove on the Far-off Terebinths."
A miktam of David,
when the Philistines seized him in Gath.

◆

2 Show me your mercy, God;
   the enemy marches over me,
   attacks me all day long.
3 My foes trample me down;
   how many fight against me!

4 When I am afraid,
   I trust you, most high God,
5 I glory in your promise,
   I trust you without fear.
   Can flesh and bone hurt me?

◆

6 All day they twist my words,
   plotting evil against me.

7 They hide themselves, lurking,
   listening for my steps,
   waiting to take my life.

8 Can nations escape their crimes?
   In your anger, God, cast them down!
9 Weigh all my turmoil,
   store up my tears;
   do you not record them all?

10 When I call to you,
   my enemies retreat.
   I am certain of this:
   God is on my side.

11 I glory in your promise, God;
   O Lord, your word I praise;
12 I trust you without fear.
   How can mortals hurt me?

◆

13 I will fulfill my vows, O God,
   offer gifts to thank you.
14 For you saved me from death,
   kept my feet from its brink.
   I walk with you, God,
   in the light of your life.   □

57

*1 For the choirmaster.
According to "Do Not Destroy." A miktam of David,
when he fled from Saul into the cave.*

◆

2 Care for me, God, take care of me,
   I have nowhere else to hide.
   Shadow me with your wings
   until all danger passes.

3 I call to the Most High,
   to God, my avenger:
4 send help from heaven to free me,
   punish those who hound me.

   Extend to me, O God,
   your love that never fails,
5 for I find myself among lions
   who crave for human flesh,
   their teeth like spears and arrows,
   their tongues sharp as swords.

6 O God, rise high above the heavens!
   Spread your glory across the earth!

◆

7 They rigged a net for me,
a trap to bring me down;
they dug a pit for me,
but they—they fell in!

8 I have decided, O God,
my decision is firm:
to you I will sing my praise.
9 Awake, my soul, to song!

Awake, my harp and lyre,
so I can wake up the dawn!
10 I will lift my voice in praise,
sing of you, Lord, to all nations.
11 For your love reaches heaven's edge,
your unfailing love, the skies.

12 O God, rise high above the heavens!
Spread your glory across the earth! □

58

**MAY GOD WIPE OUT ALL EVIL FROM THE EARTH.
LET CRIME AND VIOLENCE AND DECEIT
DISAPPEAR FROM HUMAN LIFE.**

---

*1 For the choirmaster. According to "Do Not Destroy."
A miktam of David.*

◆

2 You gods, are your verdicts just?
   Do you judge us fairly?
3 No! You rule with malice
   and measure out violence on earth.

4 The wicked do wrong from birth,
   liars go astray from the womb.
5 They are deadly as snakes,
   they are like a cobra
6 that will not hear the magic spell
   or rise for the charmer's song.

◆

7 O God, break their teeth,
   rip out the young lions' fangs.
8 Let them drain off like water,
   wither like dead grass,

9 dissolve like slugs as they crawl;
   like the stillborn, never see light.

10 God, before these thorns grow sharp,
    sweep them into the blaze.
11 The just are pleased to see vengeance done,
    they wash their feet in sinners' blood.
12 All will say, "The just win the prize!
    There is a God who judges the earth." □

59

A CHALLENGE TO GOD:
PROTECT THOSE DEVOURED BY THE POWERFUL.
GOD'S REWARD: A SONG OF GRATEFUL PRAISE.

1 *For the choirmaster. According to "Do Not Destroy."*
  A miktam of David, when Saul sent men
  to watch the house and to kill him.

◆

2 My God, rescue me from my enemies,
  raise me beyond their reach.
3 Deliver me from these villains,
  from the bloodthirsty save me.

4 See, the strong gather against me,
  they set up an ambush.
5 No crime, no fault, no sin of mine
  goads them to attack.

6 Rise up, prepare for battle,
  God of Israel.
  Lord of heaven's might,
  rise to punish the nations,
  show no mercy to traitors.

7 They come out in the dark,
  growling like dogs,
  prowling about the city.

8 Their mouths spew out evil,
  words sharp as swords.
  Who listens to them?

9 But you, Lord, just laugh,
  you mock all these nations.
10 I watch for you, my God,
  my strong tower of safety.

◆

11 Gracious God, come, help me!
  Let me look down on my foes.
12 Do not kill them all,
  or my people will forget you;
  only weaken them by your power
  and humble them, Lord, our shield.

13 Each word they mouth is sin.
   Let them be caught in their pride
   by the curses and lies they speak.

14 Destroy them in anger,
   destroy them completely!
   that all the earth may know:
   God rules in Jacob's land.

15 They come out in the dark,
   growling like dogs,
   prowling about the city.
16 They scavenge for food,
   hunting all night
   until they are filled.

17 But I celebrate your strength,
   rejoice in your love each morning,
   for you are my tower of safety,
   my haven in time of distress.

18 I sing to you, my God,
   my strong tower of safety,
   you, my faithful God.   □

psalm 59

60

1 *For the choirmaster. According to "The Lily."
A testimony. A miktam of David (for teaching),*
2 *when he fought against Aram Naharaim
and Aram Sobah,
and Joab returned and defeated
twelve thousand Edomites
in the Valley of Salt.*

3 You rejected us, God,
and breached our ranks.
You turned your fury upon us.

4 You shook the land;
it shuddered and split,
broke apart and sank.
5 You forced us to suffer,
to drink bitter wine,
to stagger in grief.

6 Raise a banner for your faithful,
unfurl it before the battle.
7 Deliver those you love,
stretch out your hand, rescue us.

◆

8 God decreed in his temple:
   "I will give away Shechem,
   in victory parcel out Succoth.
9 Manasseh and Gilead are mine.

   "With Ephraim as my helmet,
   and Judah my spear,
10 I will make Moab my wash bowl,
   trample Edom under my feet,
   and over Philistia shout in triumph."

◆

11 Who will lead us to Edom
   to breach the city wall?
12 God, will you still hold back?
   Will you desert our camp?

13 Stand by us against the enemy,
   all other aid is worthless.
14 With you the battle is ours,
   you will crush our foes.   □

61

*1 For the choirmaster. For stringed instruments.
Of David.*

◆

2 Hear me, God! I cry out,
   listen to my prayer.
3 I call from far away,
   for my courage fails.
   Lead me to a mountain height
   where I can be safe.

4 You are my refuge,
   a tower of strength against my foes.
5 Welcome me into your home,
   under your wings for ever.
6 God, you surely hear my vows;
   give me the blessings
   of those who honor your name.

◆

7 Lengthen the days of your king,
   stretch years into generations.

8 May he live with you for ever,
  secure in your faithful love.
9 I sing your name always,
  each day fulfilling my vows.   □

62

**NO PERSON, NO CREATED THING
CAN ALWAYS BE RELIED ON.
THE TRUE SECURITY IS IN GOD ALONE.**

---

1 *For the choirmaster. According to "Jeduthun."
    A psalm of David.*

2 My soul waits, silent for God,
  for God alone, my salvation,
3 alone my rock, my safety,
  my refuge: I stand secure.

4 How long will some of you attack
  tearing others down
  as if walls or fences
  on the verge of collapse?

5 You scheme to topple them,
  so smug in your lies;

your lips are all blessing,
but murder fills your heart.

◆

6 Wait, my soul, silent for God,
  for God alone, my hope,
7 alone my rock, my safety,
  my refuge: I stand secure.

8 God is my glory and safety,
  my stronghold, my haven.
9 People, give your hearts to God,
  trust always! God is our haven.

◆

10 Mortals are but a breath,
  nothing more than a mirage;
  set them on the scales,
  they prove lighter than mist.

11 Avoid extortion and fraud,
  the hopes they breed are nothing;
  and if you should grow rich,
  place no trust in wealth.

12 Time and again God said,
  "Strength and love are mine to give."
  The Lord repays us all
  in light of what we do. ☐

63

1 *A psalm of David,*
when he was in the desert of Judah.

◆

2 God, my God, you I crave;
   my soul thirsts for you,
   my body aches for you
   like a dry and weary land.
3 Let me gaze on you in your temple:
   a vision of strength and glory.

◆

4 Your love is better than life,
   my speech is full of praise.
5 I give you a lifetime of worship,
   my hands raised in your name.
6 I feast at a rich table,
   my lips sing of your glory.

7 On my bed I lie awake,
   your memory fills the night.
8 You have been my help,

I rejoice beneath your wings.
9 Yes, I cling to you,
   your right hand holds me fast.

◆

10 Let those who want me dead
   end up deep in the grave!
11 They will die by the sword,
   their bodies food for jackals.
12 But let the king find joy in God.
   All who swear the truth be praised,
   every lying mouth be shut. □

64

A DRAMATIC RESCUE!
GOD DELIVERS THE FAITHFUL FROM VIOLENCE.

1 *For the choirmaster. A psalm of David.*

◆

2 Hear my troubles, God.
   Keep me safe from terror,
3 guard me from hostile scheming
   and the rage of the violent.

4 Enemies sharpen their tongues
   and aim bitter words like arrows
5 to ambush the innocent
   with a sudden, brazen shot.

6 They polish their plans,
   conceal their traps,
   asking, "Who can see them?"
7 They hide the evil they plot.
   How devious the heart!

◆

8 God shoots an arrow,
   instantly they are struck.
9 God trips them on their own tongues.
   All who see it tremble.

10 The whole world stands in awe,
   they talk of God's work
   and ponder its meaning.
11 The just rejoice
   and find refuge in God.
   Honest hearts sing praise. ☐

65

*1 For the choirmaster.
A psalm of David; a song.*

◆

2 Praise is yours, God in Zion.
Now is the moment
to keep our vow,
3 for you, God, are listening.

All people come to you
bringing their shameful deeds.
4 You free us from guilt,
from overwhelming sin.

5 Happy are those you invite
and then welcome to your courts.
Fill us with the plenty of your house,
the holiness of your temple.

◆

6 You give victory
in answer to our prayer.

You inspire awe, God, our savior,
hope of distant lands and waters.

7 Clothed in power,
   you steady the mountains;
8 you still the roaring seas,
   restless waves, raging nations.
9 People everywhere
   stand amazed at what you do,
   east and west shout for joy.

◆

10 You tend and water the land.
   How wonderful the harvest!
   You fill your springs,
   ready the seeds, prepare the grain.

11 You soak the furrows
   and level the ridges.
   With softening rain
   you bless the land with growth.

12 You crown the year with riches.
   All you touch comes alive:
13 untilled lands yield crops,
   hills are dressed in joy,

14 flocks clothe the pastures,
   valleys wrap themselves in grain.
   They all shout for joy
   and break into song.   □

66

1 For the choirmaster. A song; a psalm.

◆

All earth, shout with joy to God!
2 Sing the glory of the Name!
Give glorious praise!
3 Say, "How awesome your works!"

Because of your mighty strength,
your enemies cringe before you.
4 All earth bows before you,
sings to you, sings to your name.

5 Come, see God's wonders,
tremendous deeds for the people:
6 God turned sea into land,
they crossed the river on foot.

Let us rejoice then in God,
7 who rules for ever with might,
keeping a watch on all nations.
Let no rebels raise their heads!

8 Bless our God, you peoples,
loudly sound God's praise,

9 who kept our spirits alive
and our feet from stumbling.

10 God, you have tested us,
refined us like silver in fire.
11 You led us into a trap,
you put a weight on our backs,
12 you let others beat us down.
We passed through water and fire,
but then you brought us relief.

◆

13 I come to your house with gifts
to keep the vow I made.
14 This promise was on my lips
when I was afflicted.
15 I will offer sacrifice,
burnt offerings of rams,
wild bulls and goats.

16 Come, listen, all who fear God,
as I tell what happened to me.
17 To God I cried aloud,
praise upon my tongue,
18 "If I have evil in my heart,
let my Lord not listen!"

19 Bless God who did listen,
heeded the sound of my prayer.
20 God did not reject my plea,
but pledged me constant love. ☐

67

1 *For the choirmaster.*
For stringed instruments. A psalm; a song.

◆

2 Favor and bless us, Lord.
  Let your face shine on us,
3 revealing your way to all peoples,
  salvation the world over.

4 Let nations sing your praise,
  every nation on earth.

◆

5 The world will shout for joy,
  for you rule the planet with justice.
  In fairness you govern the nations
  and guide the peoples of earth.

6 Let the nations sing your praise,
  every nation on earth.

◆

7 The land delivers its harvest,
God, our God, has blessed us.
8 O God, continue your blessing,
may the whole world worship you.   □

68

**THE GOD OF SINAI MARCHES FORTH.
A FESTIVE PROCESSION CELEBRATES VICTORY.
MAY GOD'S POWER SAVE A NEEDY WORLD.**

---

*1 For the choirmaster.
A psalm of David; a song.*

◆

2 God rises up,
enemies of heaven scatter:
3 they disperse like smoke,
they melt like wax,
they perish before God.

4 But the just are glad,
they rejoice before God
and celebrate with song.

psalm 68

◆

5 Sing to God's name, play hymns!
   God rides the clouds. Send up a song!
   "Lord" is God's name. Rejoice!
6 Father to the fatherless,
   defender of widows:
   God in the temple!

7 God gives the homeless a home,
   sets prisoners free to prosper,
   but the rebellious
   are banished to the wild.

◆

8 God, when you led your people,
   when you marched in the desert,
9 earth shook, heaven rained before you,
   Israel's God, the Lord of Sinai.

10 You gave us downpours
   to refresh the promised land
11 where you nourish your flock.
   Gracious God, you strengthen the weak.

◆

12 God speaks a word;
   a company of women
   spreads the good news.

13 Kings and their armies
    run and flee.
    Housewives and shepherds
    all share the plunder:
14 silver plated doves
    with bright gold wings.

15 The Almighty blew kings about
    like snow on Mount Zalmon.

◆

16 Bashan is a sacred peak,
    a mountain of high summits.
17 Soaring Bashan, why envy
    the mountain God chose as home,
    a place to live for ever?

18 With thousands and thousands
    of uncounted chariots
    the Lord came from Sinai
    to Zion's holy temple.

19 You ascended to the heights,
    you took captives
    and accepted tribute
    from those resisting you.

◆

20 Bless the Lord each day
    who carries our burden,
    who keeps us alive,

psalm 68

21 our God who saves,
our escape from death.

22 God smashed the heads of enemies,
the skulls of the guilty.
23 The Lord said:
"I bring them back from Bashan,
back from the bottom of the sea,
24 so you may tramp through their blood
and your dogs lap it up."

◆

25 People watched the procession
as you marched into your house,
my Lord, my sovereign God.
26 Singers at the head, musicians at the rear,
between them, women striking tambourines.

27 Bless God in the assembly,
all who draw water
from Israel's spring.
28 Little Benjamin leads the princes
of Judah, Zebulun, and Naphtali.

◆

29 Use your strength, God,
as you did for us in the past
30 from your house above Jerusalem.
May rulers bring you gifts!

31 Rebuke the beast of the Nile,
   wild bulls and their calves.
   Trample those who lust for silver,
   scatter the warmongers.

32 Envoys will come from Egypt,
   the Cushites will pray to God.

◆

33 Rulers of earth, sing to God.
   Make music for the Lord
34 who rides the clouds,
   whose voice is thunder.

35 Acknowledge the power of God
   who governs Israel,
   whose strength is in the stormclouds.

36 You inspire wonder
   in your temple, God of Israel,
   as you fill your people
   with power and might.

   Blessed be God!   □

69

*1 For the choirmaster.
According to "The Lilies."
Of David.*

2 Save me, God!
　Water is up to my neck.
3 I am sinking in mud,
　without a rock to stand on,
　plunged in the deep
　beneath the current.

4 I am tired of shouting,
　my throat is raw,
　my eyes swollen;
　I am worn out waiting for God.

5 Many hate me without cause,
　they outnumber the hairs on my head.
　I have fewer bones
　than I have lying enemies
　who demand I return
　what I did not steal.

◆

6 God, you know my folly,
my sins are plain to you.

7 Lord, commander of heaven's army,
may those who hope in you
not be shamed because of me.
May those seeking you
not be humbled on my account,
Lord God of Israel.

8 I bear shame and insult
because I bear your name.
9 Rejected by my family,
I am a stranger to my kin.

10 My passion for your cause
takes all my strength.
Insults meant for you
now fall on me.

11 Despite my tears and fasting,
I only gained contempt.
12 My sackcloth made me a joke.
13 I was the butt of gossips,
the victim of drunkard's taunts.

◆

14 Lord, hear this prayer,
favor me now with love,
and send me your ready help.

psalm 69

15 Lift me from the mud,
   keep me from sinking,
   let me escape my tormentors
   and rise above the waters.

16 Do not let the waters drown me,
   the deep swallow me,
   the pit close me in its mouth.
17 Answer me, Lord,
   turn to me with mercy and love.

18 Face me, I am desperate.
   Answer your servant now,
19 come to my rescue,
   free me from my enemies.

20 You know my disgrace,
   my embarrassment and shame,
   you see my oppressors.

21 Their insults break my spirit,
   I am sick at heart.
   I looked for comfort and sympathy
   but found none.
22 They poisoned my food,
   and gave me vinegar to drink.

◆

23 Make their table their trap,
   a snare for their friends.
24 Blind them,
   cripple them,

25 rage at them.
   Let your anger consume them.
26 Let their tents be deserted,
   their campsites a graveyard.

27 For they torment the sick
   and ridicule their pain.
28 Keep a full record of their guilt;
   none of your mercy for them!
29 Erase them from the book of life,
   lest they be tallied among the just.

◆

30 But I am ill, in pain.
   Rescue me, God,
   lift me up.

31 Then I shall give thanks
   and praise God's name,
32 for song pleases God more than cattle
   or bulls with horns and hooves.

33 Look and see, you oppressed,
   there is cause to rejoice
   for those who seek God.
   Let your hearts hope again,
34 for the Lord hears the poor,
   does not despise the imprisoned.

35 Praise God, heaven and earth,
   the seas and all that live in them,
36 for God rescues Zion,

rebuilds the towns of Judah
for people to own and inhabit.

37 Their offspring will inherit Judah,
and those who serve God's name
will make it their home. ☐

70

**LET EVIL COME BACK ON THOSE WHO DO EVIL,
GOOD COME BACK ON THE GOOD.**

———

1 *For the choirmaster. Of David.
For remembrance.*

2 Help me, God.
Lord, be quick to save me.
3 People are plotting to kill me;
humble them, shame them.

They want to ruin me;
ruin and disgrace them.
4 Let those who jeer at me
swallow their shameful taunts.

5 But those who seek you
and trust your saving love
rejoice and always sing,
"God is great."

6 I am poor and helpless,
O God, hurry to my side!
Lord, my help, my rescue,
do not delay. □

71

**THE LAMENT OF AN OLD PERSON
A LIFELONG FIDELITY WILL NOT BE SHAKEN.**

1 Lord, you are my shelter,
do not fail me.
2 You always do right;
deliver me, rescue me,
hear me and save me.

3 Be my rock and haven,
to whom I can always turn;
be my tower of strength,
keep me safe.
4 The ruthless and wicked trap me;
reach out to free me.

5 You are my hope, O Lord,
from the days of my youth.
6 I have relied on you since birth,
my strength from my mother's womb;
I will praise you always.

7 I am shunned like the plague,
    but you keep me in your care.
8 I am filled with your praises,
    all day I sing your glory.
9 Now I am old, my strength fails,
    do not toss me aside.

◆

10 My enemies scheme against me,
    they have designs on my life.
11 They think God has left me.
    "Strike," they say, "no one will help."

12 Do not hold back, Lord,
    run to my rescue.
13 Disgrace my accusers,
    wrap them in shame,
    make my enemies
    face utter ruin.

14 I will not lose hope,
    never stop praising you.
15 My lips speak your goodness,
    praise each day your saving acts,
    though I cannot count them all.
16 I will enter your palace proclaiming,
    "Lord God, you alone are just."

◆

17 From childhood till now
   you taught me to praise your wonders.
18 Do not leave me, Lord,
   now that I am old.

   I can still recount
   to a new generation
   your power and strength.
19 Your goodness is boundless,
   your works so great;
   who can equal you?

20 You wrack me with torment,
   but you give back my life
   and raise me from this grave.
21 You will restore my honor
   and wrap me again in mercy.

22 I will thank you, Lord,
   for your true friendship
   and play the lyre and harp for you,
   the Holy One of Israel.
23 I will sing out with joy,
   sing of how you saved me.

24 From morning till night
   I will trumpet your goodness;
   those who sought my ruin
   are defeated and shamed.   □

72

1 Of Solomon.

◆

God, give your king judgment,
the son of the king
your sense of what is right;
2 help him judge your people
and do right for the powerless.

3 May mountains bear peace,
hills bring forth justice.
4 May the king defend the poor,
set their children free,
and kill their oppressors.

◆

5 May he live as long as the sun,
as long as the moon, for ever.
6 May he be like rain on a field,
like showers that soak the earth.

7 May justice sprout in his time,
peace till the moon is no more.

psalm 72

8 May he rule from sea to sea,
   from the River to the ends of the earth.

◆

9 Enemies will cower before him,
   they will lick the dust.
10 Kings from Tarshish and the islands
   will bring their riches to him.

   Kings of Sheba, kings of Saba
   will carry gifts to him.
11 All kings will bow before him,
   all the nations serve him.

◆

12 He will rescue the poor at their call,
   those no one speaks for.
13 Those no one cares for
   he hears and will save,
14 save their lives from violence,
   lives precious in his eyes.

15 Every day they pray for him
   and bless him all his life.
   Long life to him!
   Gold to him from Saba!

16 May wheat be thick in the fields,
   fruit trees sway on the slope.
   May cities teem with people,
   thick as the forests of Lebanon.

psalm 72

17 May his name live on for ever,
   live as long as the sun.
   May all find blessing in him,
   and he be blest by all.

◆ ◆ ◆

18 Blessed be Israel's God,
   Lord of wonderful deeds!
19 Bless God's name for ever!
   Let God's glory fill the world!
   Amen and Amen!

Here end the prayers of David, son of Jesse. □

73

LIFE IS NOT FAIR.
GOOD PEOPLE SUFFER; WICKED PEOPLE PROSPER.
ONLY GOD'S PRESENCE BRINGS TRUE JOY.

1 *A psalm of Asaph.*

◆

How good God is to the just,
how faithful to the honest!

2 Yet I almost slipped,
came close to stumbling.

3 I envied the arrogant
as I watched them succeed.
4 Their bodies are perfect,
well-fed and healthy.

5 They remain untouched
by the troubles we bear.
6 They adorn themselves with pride,
wrap themselves in violence.

7 Decadent and slick,
they scheme recklessly,
8 mocking and snarling,
spewing out threats.

9 They boast the heavens are theirs,
lay claim to all the world,
10 pulling people after them,
who swallow what they say.

11 They ask, "How would God know?
Does the Most High know anything?"
12 These, then, are the wicked,
always richer, always stronger.

13 What did I gain by my clean hands,
by keeping my conscience clear?
14 I suffered day after day,
each dawn brought me pain.

15 But to talk like them
would betray your people.

psalm 73

16 I tried to fathom this,
    but it all tormented me
17 until I went to your holy place.
    Now I understand their fate.

◆

18 You set them on a slippery path,
    making them fall to their ruin.
19 How soon they are destroyed,
    swept away in terror.
20 Like images from a dream,
    you, Lord, let them fade.

21 I became embittered,
    my feelings numb;
22 I was dull, obtuse,
    stupid as an ox.
23 But I stayed close to you,
    and you took my hand.

24 You teach me wisdom,
    leading me to glory.
25 What more would I have in heaven?
    Who else delights me on earth?
26 If mind and body fail,
    you, God, are my rock,
    my support for ever.

◆

27 Those who abandon you perish;
   you destroy the unfaithful.
28 But my joy is to be near you,
   Lord God, my only refuge.
   I want to proclaim all your ways. □

74

**CAN GOD ALLOW SACRED PLACES TO BE DESTROYED
OR FAITHFUL PEOPLE TO SUFFER?
A CRY TO THE CREATOR TO RISE
IN DEFENSE OF ALL THAT BEARS GOD'S NAME.**

1 *A maskil of Asaph.*

◆

Why, God? Why always cast us off?
Why rage at the flock you tended?
2 Remember the people you chose long ago,
   those you redeemed for yourself;
   remember Zion where you dwell.

3 Walk through this total ruin,
   see their crime against your holy place:

4 when your foes shouted in the temple
   as they raised their banners.

5 They splintered paneled walls with axes
   as if chopping down trees,
6 and shattered the woodwork,
   swinging hammers and picks.

7 They defiled the dwelling place of your name,
   torched it, burned it to the ground.
8 They wanted to crush your people,
   to set all your shrines on fire.

9 There are no signs from you,
   not a single prophet
   who knows how long this will last.

10 How long, God, will they mock?
   Will they blaspheme your name for ever?
11 Why do you hold back,
   your right hand limp at your side?

◆

12 God, you have ruled from the beginning,
   bringing salvation across the earth.
13 You split the sea with might
   and smashed the heads of ocean monsters.
14 You crushed the seven-headed sea serpent,
   feeding it to the sharks.

15 You opened springs and brooks,
   you dried up rivers.

16 Yours is the day, yours the night;
   you set the moon and sun in place.
17 You fixed the regions of the earth,
   the dry and rainy seasons.

18 Remember this, Lord!
   Enemies scorn you,
   fools revile your name.
19 Do not give your dove to the hawk,
   do not neglect your poor for ever.

20 Remember the covenant,
   for the world is darkened by violence.
21 Save the downtrodden from ruin.
   Let the poor and needy praise your name.

22 Rise, O God, champion your cause!
   Fools insult you all day long.
23 Do not be deaf to their uproar,
   the constant noise of their defiance. □

75

*1 For the choirmaster.
According to "Do Not Destroy."
A psalm of Asaph; a song.*

2 We praise you, God,
 and give you thanks.
 You are present to us
 as we tell your wonders.

3 "I, your God, choose the moment
 to set things right.
4 Though earth and its people tremble,
 I secure its foundations.

5 "I say to the proud, stop boasting!
 to the wicked, stop it!
6 Stop promoting yourselves,
 pitting yourselves against the Rock."

7 No help from east or west,
 from desert or mountain,

8 for God alone judges,
   levels some, raises others.
9 The Lord holds a foaming cup,
   pours the wicked a heady wine;
   they drain it to the dregs.

◆

10 But I sing praise for ever,
   make music for the God of Jacob,
11 who breaks the power of the wicked
   and strengthens the just. ☐

76

**A HYMN TO THE WARRIOR GOD WHO DESTROYS WAR.
GOD'S POWER ALWAYS DEFENDS THE DEFENSELESS.**

1 *For the choirmaster. For stringed instruments.
A psalm of Asaph; a song.*

2 God, you are known throughout Judah,
   Israel glories in your name.
3 Your tent is pitched in Salem,
   your command post on Zion.
4 There you break flaming arrows,
   shield and sword and war itself!

5 Majestic and circled with light,
   you seize your prey;
6 stouthearted soldiers
   are stripped of their plunder.
   Dazed, they cannot lift a hand.
7 At your battle cry, God of Jacob,
   horse and rider are stunned.

8 You, the one who strikes fear—
   who can stand up to your anger!
9 Your verdict sounds from heaven;
   earth reels, then is still,
10 when you stand as judge
   to defend the oppressed.
11 When you are robed in fury,
   even the warlike give you praise.

12 Now, all you worshipers,
   keep your promise to God,
   bring gifts to the Holy One
13 who terrifies princes
   and stuns the rulers of earth.   □

77

**THE GOD WHO ONCE WORKED WONDERS
SEEMS ABSENT OR EVEN POWERLESS.
PERHAPS PRAISE FOR PAST MARVELS
WILL MOVE GOD TO RESCUE ONCE AGAIN.**

*1 For the choirmaster. According to "Jeduthun."
A psalm of Asaph.*

◆

2 I cry to you, God! I plead with you!
　If only you would hear me!

3 By day I seek you in my distress,
　by night I raise my hands in prayer,
　but my spirit refuses comfort.
4 I groan when I remember you;
　when I think of you, I grow faint.

5 You keep me from sleep.
　Troubled, I cannot speak.
6 I consider former days,
　the years gone by;
7 all night, memories fill my heart,
　I brood and question.

8 Will God always reject me?
　Never again be pleased?
9 Has God stopped loving me

and cut me off for ever?
10 Can God forget to pity,
    can anger block God's mercy?

◆

11 It troubles me to think
    the Almighty has grown weak.
12 I recall your awesome deeds,
    your wonders of old.
13 I reflect on all you have done,
    on all your works.

14 You alone are holy.
    What god compares to you?
15 You are the God of power,
    strong among the nations.
16 You reached out to save your people,
    the children of Jacob and Joseph.

◆

17 Seeing you, the waters churned,
    shuddering, writhing,
    convulsed to the depths.
18 Clouds poured down rain,
    thunder shook the heavens,
    lightning darted like arrows.

19 And the thunder rolled,
    flashes lit up the world,
    the earth trembled and quaked.

20 You set a path through the sea,
   a way through raging waters,
   with no trace of your footprints.

21 You led your flock
   under Moses and Aaron.   □

78

A WISDOM PSALM.
BY TELLING GOD'S GOODNESS AND OUR FRAILTY
FUTURE GENERATIONS WILL REMEMBER
AND LEARN TO TRUST GOD.

---

1 *A maskil of Asaph.*

◆

Listen, my people,
mark each word.
2 I begin with a story,
I speak of mysteries
welling up from ancient depths,
3 heard and known from our elders.

4 We must not hide
this story from our children

but tell the mighty works
and all the wonders of God.
5 The Lord gave precepts to Jacob,
instructions to Israel,
that the people before us
could teach their children.

6 Let future generations learn
and let them grow up
to teach their young
7 to trust in God,
remembering great deeds,
cherishing the law.

8 Not like their ancestors,
stubborn, bitter, wavering,
unfaithful to God;
9 not like the Ephraimites,
archers who fled the battle,
10 breaking their covenant,
defying the Lord.

11 They forgot all God had done,
wonders revealed to them.

◆

12 Their ancestors beheld
the wonders of God
in the land of Egypt,
on the fields of Tanis.

13 God divided the waters,
   walled back the sea
   and led them through,
14 a cloud to guide them by day,
   glowing fire by night.

15 God split desert rocks
   to quench their thirst
   with water from the deep.
16 Streams gushed forth,
   flowing like rivers.

17 Yet they kept on sinning,
   defying the Most High in the desert.
18 Willfully they tested God,
   demanding the food they craved.
19 They complained,
   "Can God spread a feast
   even in this wasteland?"

20 Yes, God struck rock
   and water flowed,
   but they dared to ask,
   "Is there bread and meat
   to feed this people?"

21 Hearing this, the Lord seethed,
   breathing fire against Jacob,
   flaring up against Israel,
22 for they had no faith,
   no trust in God's power to save.

23 God spoke from above:
   The skies opened,
24 raining down manna,
   bread from the heavens.
25 God gave them plenty,
   they ate a giant's portion.

26 A blistering wind from the east,
   a strong wind from the south
27 scattered meat like driven dust
   and quail like the blown sand,
28 falling in the middle of the camp,
   all around the tents.

29 The people stuffed their mouths,
   God satisfied their greed.
30 But while they gorged themselves,
   cramming down their food,
31 God's anger flared against them,
   destroying their sturdiest,
   striking down Israel's youth.

32 Yet they kept on sinning,
   blind to the wonders of God.

33 Their days vanished like breath,
   their years ended in terror.
34 As some died, others began to pray.
   Repenting, they reached out,
35 remembering their rock,
   God Most High, their redeemer.

36 But false and deceitful,
   they lied to God.
37 Ungrateful, disloyal,
   they betrayed the covenant.

38 Yet God, in compassion,
   did not destroy them,
   but held back anger,
   restrained fury,
   forgave their sin.
39 God remembered their weakness,
   flesh as fragile as breath.

◆

40 How often they rebelled,
   grieving God in the barren desert,
41 for ever putting God on trial,
   tormenting the Holy One of Israel.

42 They forgot God's power,
   that day of deliverance,
43 when God gave signs in Egypt,
   wonders in the fields of Tanis.

44 God polluted Egypt's streams
   turning water to blood.
45 God sent hungry flies
   and destructive frogs,
46 handed crops to the worm,
   the harvest to locusts.

47 God struck vines with hail,
fig trees with frost,
48 hurling hail at cattle,
lightning bolts at sheep.

49 Seething, raging with fury,
God sent strife and destruction
as messengers of doom,
50 leveled a path for death,
cast a plague upon their cattle,
51 and slew the firstborn of Egypt,
so that none were spared.

52 Like a flock led safely through the desert,
53 God led Israel without fear,
while their enemies drowned in the sea.

54 They were led to God's sacred land,
the mountain claimed by the Lord.
55 God dislodged the nations
and divided their inheritance;
Israel took over their tents.

56 Still, they tested God,
spurning the decrees of the Most High,
57 turning fickle like their ancestors,
unsteady as a faulty bow.
58 They built shrines in high places,
carved images to provoke God.

59 God was enraged
and cast off Israel.
60 God deserted Shiloh,
no longer at home with this people.

61 God abandoned the ark,
   letting it fall captive.
62 God condemned Israel to the sword,
   angered with his people.

63 War devoured the young men —
   no bridal songs for maidens.
64 Swords cut down the priests —
   no dirges from their widows.

65 Stirring from sleep
   like a warrior shaking off wine,
66 God attacked them like foes,
   heaping shame on them.

67 God rejected Joseph,
   put Ephraim aside,
68 choosing the tribe of Judah,
   looking with love on Zion.
69 God built his sanctuary,
   high as the heavens,
   steady as the earth.

70 David was chosen God's servant,
   called from the sheepfold
71 and brought from his flocks
   to shepherd God's people Jacob.
72 David tended them with care,
   David led them with a firm hand.   □

79

1 A psalm of Asaph.

◆

Nations overrun your estate, O God;
   they defile your temple and destroy Jerusalem.

2 Your dead servants are thrown to vultures,
   the bodies of the holy to scavengers.
3 Their blood streams through Jerusalem,
   no one is left to bury them.

4 We are laughed at by neighbors,
   the object of mockery and scorn.
5 How long, O Lord?
   Will you always be angry?
   Will your passion consume us like fire?

◆

6 Vent your anger on faithless nations,
   on regimes that ignore your name,
7 for they ate Jacob alive
   and devastated his home.

8 Do not make us pay
for the sins of our parents
but welcome us with love.
We are left with nothing.

9 Live up to the name of Savior.
Rescue us, forgive our sins,
keep your own good name.

10 Do not let the nations taunt us,
"Where is their God?"
Show them before our eyes
how you avenge the blood of your servants.

11 Heed the prisoner's groan,
use your power to save the condemned.
12 Repay our neighbors seven times
for the way they abused you, Lord.

◆

13 We, your own people,
the flock in your pasture,
will give unending thanks.
In every age to come
we will sing your praise.   □

80

*1 For the choirmaster.
According to "The Lilies."
A testimony. A psalm of Asaph.*

◆

2 Hear us, Shepherd of Israel,
  leader of Joseph's flock.
3 From your throne on the cherubim
  shine out for Ephraim,
  for Benjamin and Manasseh.
  Gather your strength,
  come, save us!

4 Restore to us, God,
  the light of your presence,
  and we shall be saved.

◆

5 How long, Lord God of might,
  will you smoulder with rage,
  despite our prayers?

6 For bread you feed us tears,
   we drink them by the barrel.
7 You let our neighbors mock,
   our enemies scorn us.

8 Restore to us, God of might,
   the light of your presence,
   and we shall be saved.

◆

9 You brought a vine from Egypt,
   cleared out nations to plant it;
10 you prepared the ground
   and made it take root
   to fill the land.

11 It overshadowed the mountains,
   towered over the mighty cedars,
12 stretched its branches to the sea,
   its roots to the distant river.

13 Why have you now torn down its walls?
   All who pass by steal the grapes,
14 wild boars tear up its roots,
   beasts devour its fruit.

15 Turn our way, God of might,
   look down from heaven;
   tend this vine you planted,
16 cherish it once more.
17 May those who slashed and burned it
   wither at your rebuke.

◆

18 Rest your hand upon your chosen one
   who draws strength from you.
19 We have not turned from you.
   Give us life again
   and we will invoke your name.

20 Restore to us, Lord God of might,
   the light of your presence,
   and we shall be saved. □

81

A FESTIVAL PSALM CELEBRATING GOD'S LAW.
TO HEAR GOD'S WORD IS TO BE SUSTAINED
WITH SWEETNESS AND LIFE.

1 *For the choirmaster. Upon the gittith. Of Asaph.*

◆

2 Shout joy to God,
   the God of our strength,
   sing to the God of Jacob.

3 Lift hearts, strike tambourines,
   sound lyre and harp.

4 Blow trumpets at the New Moon,
 till the full moon of our feast.

5 For this is a law for Israel,
 the command of Jacob's God,
6 decreed for the house of Joseph
 when we marched from Egypt.

◆

We heard a voice unknown:
7 "I lifted burdens from your backs,
 a blistering load from your hands.

8 "You cried out in pain
 and I rescued you;
 robed in thunder,
 I answered you.
 At the waters of Meribah
 I tested you.

9 "My people, hear my complaint;
 Israel, if you would only listen.
10 You shall have no other gods,
 do not bow before them.
11 I am the Lord your God.
 I brought you out of Egypt
 and fed your hungry mouths.

12 "But you would not hear me,
 my people rejected me.
13 So I hardened your hearts,
 and you left me out of your plans.

14 My people, if you would only listen!
   Israel, walk in my ways!

15 "Then I will strike your enemy,
   and put them all to flight.
16 With their fate sealed,
   my foes will grovel at your feet.
17 But you, O Israel,
   will feast on finest wheat,
   will savor pure wild honey." □

82

**WHAT IS THE PURPOSE OF POWER?
UNLIKE ALL OTHER POWERS,
GOD'S POWER IS ALWAYS AT THE SERVICE
OF THE NEEDY AND OPPRESSED.**

1 *A psalm of Asaph.*

◆

God stands in heaven's court
to judge all other gods:
2 "How long will you gods
pervert the truth
and side with the wicked?

3 "Hand down justice
   to orphans and the weak,
   uphold the rights
   of the poor and oppressed.
4 Free the weak and needy
   from the grip of the wicked."

◆

5 These gods know nothing,
   they wander in the dark
   while the world falls to pieces.

6 "I had thought of you as gods,
   born of highest heaven,
   but you will die like any creature
   and fall like any prince."

◆

7 Rise, God, judge the world.
   All nations are yours.   □

psalm 82

83

**A CRY TO GOD FOR HELP
AGAINST A COALITION OF POWERFUL ENEMIES
BENT ON ANNIHILATING GOD'S PEOPLE.
HOW WILL GOD WIN THE VICTORY?**

---

1 A song; a psalm of Asaph.

◆

2 God, do not be deaf,
  do not be still,
  do not be mute.

◆

3 Listen to the uproar
  of your enemies.
  Those who despise you
  rise up in revolt.

4 They devise clever plots
  against your people,
  they scheme
  against those you treasure.

5 They say:
  "Let us wipe out
  the nation of Israel
  until its name is forgotten."

6 They conspire as one,
  swear a covenant against you:

7 Edom and Ishmael,
  Moab and Hagar,
8 Gebal and Ammon and Amalek,
  Philistia and Tyre.
9 Even Assyria joins them
  to increase the forces
  of Lot's children.

◆

10 Crush them like Midian,
  like Sisera,
  like Jabin at the stream of Kishon.
11 Destroyed at Endor,
  they became dung
  for the ground.

12 Make their nobles
  like Oreb and Zeeb,
  all their leaders
  like Zebah and Zalmunna,
13 who said,
  "Let us seize God's pastureland."

14 Reduce them, God,
  to tumbleweed,
  to straw in the wind.

15 As a fire burns a forest
  or a flame ignites a mountain,

16 chase them down
   with your storm,
   terrify them with a gale.

17 Shame them, Lord,
   into honoring your name.
18 Humble them,
   terrify them;
   let them die in disgrace.

19 All this to make them know
   you are the only one
   whose name is Lord,
   supreme above the earth.   □

84

WHERE GOD DWELLS IS DEARER THAN ANY OTHER HOME.

1 *For the choirmaster. Upon the gittith.*
   A psalm of the sons of Korah.

2 Your temple is my joy,
   Lord of heaven's might.
3 I am eager for it,

eager for the courts of God.
My flesh, my flesh sings
its joy to the living God.

4 As a sparrow homing,
a swallow seeking a nest
to hatch its young,
I am eager for your altars,
Lord of heaven's might,
my king, my God.

◆

5 To live with you is joy,
to praise you and never stop.
6 Those you bless with courage
will bless you from their hearts.

7 When they cross the Valley of Thirst
the ground is spaced with springs,
with the welcome rain of autumn.
8 They travel the towns to reach
the God of gods in Zion.

◆

9 Hear me, Lord of might,
heed me, God of Jacob.
10 God our shield, look,
see the face of your anointed.

11 One day within your courts
is worth a thousand without.

I would rather stand at God's gate
than move among the wicked.

12 God is our sun, our shield,
the giver of honor and grace.
The Lord never fails to bless
those who walk with integrity.
13 Lord of heaven's might,
blest are all who trust in you.   □

85

A SONG IN TWO PARTS:
A PLEA TO GOD TO RESTORE THE PEOPLE'S LIFE;
AN ORACLE PROMISING THE ARRIVAL OF PEACE.

———

*1 For the choirmaster.
A psalm of the sons of Korah.*

2 Lord, you loved your land,
brought Jacob back,
3 forgot our guilt,
forgave our sins,
4 swallowed your anger,
your blazing anger.

5 Bring us back,
  saving God.
  End your wrath.
6 Will it stop,
  or drag on for ever?

7 Turn, revive us,
  nourish our joy.
8 Show us mercy,
  save us, Lord!

◆

9 I listen to God speaking:
  "I, the Lord, speak peace,
  peace to my faithful people
  who turn their hearts to me."
10 Salvation is coming near,
  glory is filling our land.

11 Love and fidelity embrace,
  peace and justice kiss.
12 Fidelity sprouts from the earth,
  justice leans down from heaven.

13 The Lord pours out riches,
  our land springs to life.
14 Justice clears God's path,
  justice points the way. □

86

1 A prayer of David.

◆

Hear me, Lord, and act,
I am poor and helpless.
2 You are my God,
watch over me,
for I am loyal to you.
Save me, your servant,
for I trust you.

3 Each waking hour
I beg your mercy, Lord.
4 Bring joy to me, your servant,
I offer myself to you.
5 You are good and forgiving,
loyal to all who call on you.

◆

6 Hear my prayer, O Lord,
answer my cry for help.
7 In my despair I plead,
knowing you will act.

8 No god can match you, Lord,
you outdo all others.

9 Every nation you formed
will come to worship
and honor your name.
10 You are mighty
and work great wonders.
You alone are God!

◆

11 Mark your path, Lord,
that I may follow your truth.
Make my one desire
to revere your name.

12 With all I am, I thank you, God,
and honor your name for ever.
13 Your love for me is great,
it saves me from the grave.

14 The proud rise against me,
brutal gangs seek my life,
with no thought of you.
15 But you are Lord of mercy and care,
a God slow to anger,
full of loyalty and love.

16 Turn to me, pity me,
strengthen your daughter's child,
rescue your servant.

17 Show me a sign of your love
  to shock and disgrace my enemy.
  Bring me help and comfort, Lord. □

87

THE SEARCH FOR HOME IS DEEP IN EVERY PERSON.
THE SEARCH IS FOR JERUSALEM.

1 *A psalm of the sons of Korah; a song.*

  Zion is set on the holy mountain.
2 The Lord loves her gates
  above all the dwellings of Israel.
3 Great is your renown, city of God.

4 I register as her citizens
  Egypt and Babylon,
  Philistia, Ethiopia, and Tyre:
  "Each one was born in her."

5 People will say, "Zion mothered
  each and every one."
  The Most High protects the city.

6 God records in the register,
  "This one was born here."
7 Then people will dance and sing,
  "My home is here!" □

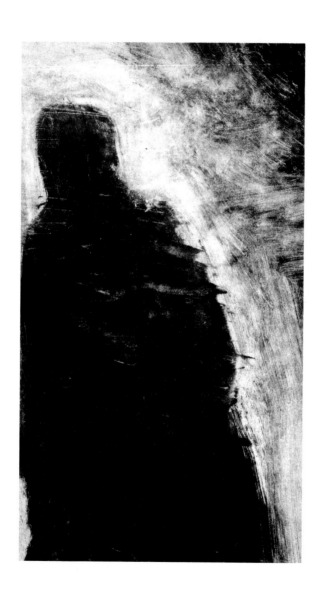

88

1 A song. A psalm of the sons of Korah.
For the choirmaster. According to "Mahalath."
For singing; a maskil of Heman the Ezrahite.

◆

2 Save me, Lord my God!
 By day, by night, I cry out.
3 Let my prayer reach you;
 turn, listen to me.

◆

4 I am steeped in trouble,
 ready for the grave.
5 I am like one destined for the pit,
 a warrior deprived of strength,
6 forgotten among the dead,
 buried with the slaughtered
 for whom you care no more.

7 You tossed me to the bottom of the pit,
 into its murky darkness,

8 your anger pulled me down
like roaring waves.

9 You took my friends away,
disgraced me before them.
Trapped here with no escape,
10 I cannot see beyond my pain.

Lord, I cry out to you all day,
my hands keep reaching out.
11 Do you work marvels for the dead?
Can shadows rise and sing praise?

12 Is your mercy sung in the grave,
your lasting love in Sheol?
13 Are your wonders known in the pit?
your justice, in forgotten places?

14 But I cry out to you, God,
each morning I plead with you.
15 Why do you reject me, Lord?
Why do you hide your face?

16 Weak since childhood,
I am often close to death.
Your torments track me down,
17 your rage consumes me,
your trials destroy me.

psalm 88

18 All day, they flood around me,
   pressing down, closing me in.
19 You took my friends from me,
   darkness is all I have left. □

89

**THE FAITHFUL GOD,
WHO HOLDS UP SKIES, STARS, ALL CREATION,
WILL SURELY HONOR THE PROMISE TO DAVID.**

---

1 *A maskil of Ethan the Ezrahite.*

2 I sing your love all my days, Lord,
   your faithfulness, from age to age.
3 I know your love is unending,
   your fidelity outlasts the heavens.

4 "I, God, covenant with my chosen one,
   I swear to David, my servant,
5 to establish your house for ever,
   to uphold your throne, from age to age."

◆

6 The skies tell your wonders, Lord,
   the stars, your constant love.
7 In the heavens what equals you?
   What god compares with you?

8 Great and dreaded God,
   you strike terror among the holy ones.
9 Who is like you, Lord of might,
   clothed in truth, a God of power?

10 You rule the storming seas,
   you calm the roaring waves.
11 Yes! You split the sea monster
   and scatter your enemies.

12 Yours the sky, yours the earth,
   yours the world of creatures.
13 You created north and south.
   Mount Tabor and Mount Hermon
   sing out your name.

14 Yours, a mighty arm,
   yours, a powerful hand
   raised in triumph.
15 Justice and right anchor your throne,
   fidelity and love attend you.

16 How your people rejoice!
   you summon us into your light.
17 Lord, your name is our joy,
   and your justice, our strength.

psalm 89

18 You, our glory and power,
     favor us with victory,
19 you, the Holy One of Israel,
     our shield, our Lord, our king.

◆

20 In a vision, O God,
     you speak to your beloved:
     "I help this warrior,
     chosen from the people.
21 I seek out David, my servant,
     and anoint him with sacred oil.

22 "My hand strengthens him,
     my arm encircles him.
23 No enemy ensnares him,
     no schemer brings him down.

24 "I crush his foes,
     I strike those who hate him.
25 I pledge loyalty and love;
     in my name, I raise him up.
26 I extend his hand over the sea,
     his right hand over the mighty oceans.

27 "He calls out to me: 'My father,
     my God, my rock of safety!'
28 I respond: 'My firstborn,
     noblest of kings.'

29 "I honor my pledge of love,
     guard my covenant for ever.

30 I establish his royal house,
   his throne firm as the heavens.

31 "Should his children desert my laws
   and abandon my ways,
32 should they violate my precepts
   and not respect my laws,
33 I shall punish their rebellion
   with a rod and a scourge.

34 "But I shall not withdraw my love
   or fail to be faithful.
35 I will not break my covenant
   or revoke my word.

36 "Bound by my holiness,
   I cannot lie to David.
37 His house will last for ever,
   his throne like the sun,
38 constant as the moon,
   everlasting as the sky."

◆

39 But you, God, become angry,
   rejecting, despising your anointed one.
40 You spurn the covenant with your servant,
   you drag his crown in the dust.
41 You break through his defenses,
   batter down his strongholds.

42 People roam and plunder,
   neighbors scorn.

psalm 89

43 Hate has the upper hand,
   enemies rejoice.

44 You blunt his sword,
   useless now for battle.
45 You end his glory,
   cast his throne to the ground.
46 You cut short his youth,
   cover him with shame.

◆

47 How long, O Lord?
   Must you hide for ever,
   seething with anger?
48 Remember me — how short my life!
   Do you create people for nothing?

49 Who lives and never dies?
   Who escapes the hand of death?
50 Where, Lord, is that ancient love,
   faithfully sworn to David?

51 Recall how they insulted your servant,
   how I bore the taunts of nations.
52 Your enemies hurl shame, Lord!
   They shame your anointed!

53 Blessed be God for ever. Amen. Amen.   □

psalm 89

90

1 A prayer of Moses, man of God.

◆

You have been our haven, Lord,
from generation to generation.
2 Before the mountains existed,
before the earth was born,
from age to age you are God.

3 You return us to dust,
children of earth back to earth.
4 For in your eyes a thousand years
are like a single day:
they pass with the swiftness of sleep.

5 You sweep away the years
as sleep passes at dawn,
6 like grass that springs up in the day
and is withered by evening.

◆

7 For we perish at your wrath,
  your anger strikes terror.
8 You lay bare our sins
  in the piercing light of your presence.
9 All our days wither beneath your glance,
  our lives vanish like a breath.

10 Our life is a mere seventy years,
   eighty with good health,
   and all it gives us
   is toil and distress;
   then the thread breaks
   and we are gone.

11 Who can know the force of your anger?
   Your fury matches our fear.
12 Teach us to make use of our days
   and bring wisdom to our hearts.

◆

13 How long, O Lord, before you return?
   Pity your servants,
14 shine your love on us each dawn,
   and gladden all our days.

15 Balance our past sorrows
   with present joys
16 and let your servants, young and old,
   see the splendor of your work.

17 Let your loveliness shine on us,
   and bless the work we do,
   bless the work of our hands. □

91

**A NIGHT PRAYER.
GOD'S PROTECTION IS DEFENSE AGAINST DANGER.
GOD PROMISES LIFE TO THOSE WHO TRUST.**

---

1 All you sheltered by the Most High,
   who live in Almighty God's shadow,
2 say to the Lord, "My refuge, my fortress,
   my God in whom I trust!"

3 God will free you from hunters' snares,
   will save you from deadly plague,
4 will cover you like a nesting bird.
   God's wings will shelter you.

5 No nighttime terror shall you fear,
   no arrows shot by day,
6 no plague that prowls the dark,
   no wasting scourge at noon.

7 A thousand may fall at your side,
   ten thousand at your right hand.

But you shall live unharmed:
God is sturdy armor.

8 You have only to open your eyes
to see how the wicked are repaid.
9 You have the Lord as refuge,
have made the Most High your stronghold.

10 No evil shall ever touch you,
no harm come near your home.
11 God instructs angels
to guard you wherever you go.

12 With their hands they support you,
so your foot will not strike a stone.
13 You will tread on lion and viper,
trample tawny lion and dragon.

◆

14 "I deliver all who cling to me,
raise the ones who know my name,
15 answer those who call me,
stand with those in trouble.
These I rescue and honor,
16 satisfy with long life,
and show my power to save." ☐

92

1 A psalm; a song for the sabbath day.

2 How good to thank you, Lord,
to praise your name, Most High,
3 to sing your love at dawn,
your faithfulness at dusk
4 with sound of lyre and harp,
with music of the lute.
5 For your work brings delight,
your deeds invite song.

6 I marvel at what you do.
Lord, how deep your thought!
7 Fools do not grasp this,
nor the senseless understand.
8 Scoundrels spring up like grass,
flourish and quickly wither.
9 You, Lord, stand firm for ever.

10 See how your enemies perish,
scattered to the winds,
11 while you give me brute strength,
pouring rich oil upon me.
12 I have faced my enemies,
heard them plot against me.

13 The just grow tall like palm trees,
   majestic like cedars of Lebanon.
14 They are planted in the temple courts
   and flourish in God's house,
15 green and heavy with fruit
   even in old age.

16 Proclaim that God is just,
   my rock without a fault.   □

93

**NO CHAOS, DISASTER OR MALICE,
CAN THREATEN GOD'S REIGN.**

1 Lord, you reign with glory,
  draped in splendor, girt with power.
  The world stands firm,
  not to be shaken,
2 for your throne, ageless God,
  has stood from of old.

3 Onward roll the waves, O God,
  onward like thunder,
  onward like fury.
4 Thundering above the waters,
  high above ocean breakers,
  you, God, rise with might.

5 Your decrees stand unshaken;
  the beauty of holiness
  fills your house for ever, Lord.   □

94

WILL GOD NOT RISE UP AGAINST EVIL?
A PRAYER OF CONFIDENCE:
GOD'S FAITHFULNESS NEVER WAVERS.

1 Lord, avenging God,
  avenging God, reveal yourself!
2 Rise up, judge of the earth,
  give the arrogant what they deserve.

3 How long, God, how long
  will the wicked strut around?
4 They bluster and boast,
  flaunting their devious ways.

5 Lord, they trample your people,
  they wreck your heritage.
6 They kill widows and strangers,
  they murder orphans.
7 "The Lord is blind," they say.
  "The God of Jacob sees nothing."

8 Take note, you fools,
　 you stupid people!
　 When will you understand?
9 Does God, who made ears,
　 not hear?
　 Does God, who made eyes,
　 not see?

10 Does God, who corrects the nations,
　 not punish?
　 who teaches humankind,
　 lack knowledge?
11 The Lord knows our thoughts,
　 knows how empty they are.

12 Blest are those you instruct, God,
　 those you teach your law;
13 they find comfort in evil times,
　 till a grave is dug for the wicked.

14 You never desert your people, Lord,
　 never abandon your chosen.
15 Right and justice will return,
　 bringing peace to the honest.

◆

16 Who speaks for me against the wicked?
　 Who sides with me against evildoers?
17 Without your help, Lord,
　 I would lie silent in the grave.

18 When I feel myself slipping,
   your love supports me, Lord.
19 When I am weighed down by worries,
   your care lifts my spirit.

20 Do you side with corrupt officials,
   who use law to burden others?
21 They plot against the just,
   condemning the innocent to death.

22 You, Lord, my strength,
   my God, my rock of safety,
23 you turn their evil against them;
   their own deeds destroy them.
   The Lord our God destroys them.   □

95

**PRAISE THE MIGHTY CREATOR
WHO IS ALSO A CARING SHEPHERD.
FAILURE TO HEAR GOD'S VOICE BRINGS DISASTER.**

1 Come, sing with joy to God,
  shout to our savior, our rock.
2 Enter God's presence with praise,
  enter with shouting and song.

3 A great God is the Lord,
  over the gods like a king.
4 God cradles the depths of the earth,
  holds fast the mountain peaks.
5 God shaped the ocean and owns it,
  formed the earth by hand.

6 Come, bow down and worship,
  kneel to the Lord our maker.
7 This is our God, our shepherd,
  we are the flock led with care.

◆

8 Listen today to God's voice:
  "Harden no heart as at Meribah,
  on that day in the desert at Massah.
9 There your people tried me,
  though they had seen my work.

10 "Forty years with that lot!
   I said: They are perverse,
   they do not accept my ways.
11 So I swore in my anger:
   They shall not enter my rest." □

96

SING AND SING AND SING!
ALL CREATION SINGS THE PRAISE OF GOD
WHO FILLS THE WORLD WITH VIBRANT LIFE.

1 A new song for the Lord!
　Sing it and bless God's name,
2 everyone, everywhere!
3 Tell the whole world
　God's triumph day to day,
　God's glory, God's wonder.

◆

4 A noble God deserving praise,
　the dread of other gods,
5 the puny gods of pagans;
　for our God made the heavens—
6 the Lord of majestic light
　who fills the temple with beauty.

◆

7 Proclaim the Lord, you nations,
　praise the glory of God's power,
8 praise the glory of God's name!
　Bring gifts to the temple,
9 bow down, all the earth,
　tremble in God's holy presence.

psalm 96

10 Tell the nations, "The Lord rules!"
   As the firm earth is not swayed,
   nothing can sway God's judgment.
11 Let heaven and earth be glad,
   the sea and sea creatures roar,
12 the field and its beasts exult.

   Then let the trees of the forest sing
13 before the coming of the Lord,
   who comes to judge the nations,
   to set the earth aright,
   restoring the world to order.   □

97

**A PARADOXICAL PICTURE:
THE TERRIFYING MAJESTY OF GOD BRINGS JOY
TO THOSE WHO LOVE THE LORD.**

1 The Lord rules: the earth is eager,
   joy touches distant lands.
2 God is wrapped in thunder cloud,
   throned on justice, throned on right.

3 Fire marches out in front
   and burns up all resistance.
4 Overhead, God's lightning flares,
   the earth shudders to see it.

5 Mountains melt down like wax
  before the Lord, the ruler of all.
6 Overhead God's justice resounds,
  a glory all people can see.

◆

7 Idolators are the fools,
  they brag of empty gods.
  You gods, be subject to the Lord!
8 Zion hears, and is happy.
  The cities of Judah are joyful
  about your judgments, Lord.

9 You, Lord, you reach high
  in majesty above the earth,
  far higher than any god.
10 Those who love the Lord hate evil;
  God shields their faithful lives
  and breaks the hold of the wicked.

11 Light will rain down on the just,
  joy on the loyal heart.
12 Be joyous in the Lord God,
  you people of faith,
  praise God's holy name!   □

98

GOD DELIVERS THE COVENANT PEOPLE FROM DEATH.
THE VICTORY IS EVIDENCE THAT GOD'S RULE
WILL BRING PEACE AND LIFE TO ALL CREATION.

1 A psalm.

◆

Sing to the Lord a new song,
the Lord of wonderful deeds.
Right hand and holy arm
brought victory to God.

2 God made that victory known,
revealed justice to nations,
3 remembered a merciful love
loyal to the house of Israel.
The ends of the earth have seen
the victory of our God.

◆

4 Shout to the Lord, you earth,
break into song, into praise!
5 Sing praise to God with a harp,
with a harp and sound of music.
6 With sound of trumpet and horn,
shout to the Lord, our king.

◆

7 Let the sea roar with its creatures,
  the world and all that live there!
8 Let rivers clap their hands,
  the hills ring out their joy!

9 The Lord our God comes,
  comes to rule the earth,
  justly to rule the world,
  to govern the peoples aright.   □

99

**THROUGH TIME, THROUGH THE WHOLE WORLD
PEOPLE ACCLAIM GOD'S RULE.
HERE IN THIS HOLY PLACE SING PRAISE!**

1 The Lord reigns from the cherubim throne,
  nations tremble, earth shakes!
2 The Lord of Zion is great,
  high above all peoples.
3 Praise the great and fearful name,
  "Holy is the Lord!"

◆

4 Almighty ruler, you love justice,
   you strengthen the upright
   and secure equity for Jacob.
5 Bow down to worship at God's feet,
   lift your voice in praise,
   "Holy is the Lord!"

◆

6 First among priests of the Lord
   were Moses, Aaron, and Samuel;
   they called out God's Name.
   The Lord heard them
7 and spoke from a pillar of cloud;
   they honored each command.

8 Our God did what was needed,
   it was yours, Lord, to punish,
   yours to forgive sin.
9 Bow down to worship the Lord,
   give praise in God's holy place,
   "Holy is the Lord our God!" □

100

A PERFECT DANCE OF THANKSGIVING.
GOD'S PEOPLE GATHER FROM THE WHOLE EARTH
TO ENTER THE TEMPLE GATES IN PROCESSION
AND PRAISE THE GOD WHO IS LASTING LOVE.

1 A psalm of thanksgiving.

Shout joy to the Lord, all earth,
2 serve the Lord with gladness,
enter God's presence with joy!

3 Know that the Lord is God,
our maker to whom we belong,
our shepherd, and we the flock.

4 Enter the temple gates,
the courtyard with thanks and praise;
give thanks and bless God's name.

5 Indeed the Lord is good!
God's love is for ever,
faithful from age to age.   □

101

SEEK RIGHT BEHAVIOR,
THE JUSTICE AND TRUTH OF GOD,
WHILE ACTIVELY REJECTING ALL THAT IS EVIL.

---

1 A psalm of David.

I sing to you, O Lord,
sing your justice and love,
2 and live the truth I sing.
When will you come to me?

I show my royal household
how to lead a perfect life.
3 I shun what is devious
and hate deceit—
it can never touch me.

4 The wicked dare not approach me,
for I am no friend to evil.
5 I silence those who gossip,
I detest their vanity and pride.

6 I look for loyal people
to share my palace.
Those who live honest lives
will serve me.

7 I cannot bear scoundrels and liars,
they are not welcome in my house.

8 My daily work
is to rid the land of evil
and cleanse the City of God. □

102

**THE CRY OF DESPAIR TURNS TO PRAISE.
GOD WHO SEES AND HEARS ALL THINGS
IS MOVED TO COMPASSION.**

---

1 *The prayer of someone who is faint
and pours out complaints to the Lord.*

◆

2 Hear my prayer, Lord,
let my cry reach you.
3 Do not turn from me
in my hour of need.
When I call, listen,
answer me at once.

4 For my days dissolve like smoke,
my bones are burned to ash.
5 My heart withers away like grass.
I even forget to eat,
6 so consumed am I with grief.
My skin hangs on my bones.

7 Like a gull lost in the desert,
   like an owl haunting the ruins,
8 I keep a solitary watch,
   a lone bird on a roof.
9 All day my enemies mock me,
   they make my name a curse.

10 For bread, I eat ashes,
   tears salt my drink.
11 You lifted me up in anger
   and threw me to the ground.
12 My days pass into evening,
   I wither like the grass.

◆

13 But you, Lord, preside for ever,
   every age remembers you.
14 Rise with mercy for Zion,
   for now is the time for pity.
15 Your servants treasure every stone,
   they cherish even the rubble.

16 Nations will fear your name,
   your glory will humble kings.
17 When you rebuild Zion's walls,
   you will appear in glory, Lord.
18 You hear the homeless pleading
   and do not mock their prayer.

19 Write this down for those to come,
   a people created to praise our God:

psalm 102

20 "The Lord watches from on high,
   searches the earth from heaven.

21 "God hears the prisoner's groan
   and sets the doomed free
22 to sing the Lord's name in Zion,
   God's praise in Jerusalem.
23 There the nations and peoples
   gather to serve the Lord."

◆

24 God has broken me in my prime,
   has cut short my days.
25 I say: "My God, do not take me.
   My life is only half-spent,
   while you live from age to age."

26 Long ago you made the earth,
   the heavens, too, are your work.
27 Should they decay, you remain.
   Should they wear out like a robe,
   like clothing changed and thrown away,
28 you are still the same.
   Your years will never end.

29 May your servants' line last for ever,
   our children grow strong before you.   □

103

**A BLESSING CUP, OVERFLOWING WITH GRATITUDE:
FROM GOD IS OUR HEALING AND FORGIVENESS,
FROM GOD IS TENDERNESS AND MERCY.**

---

1 *Of David.*

◆

My soul, bless the Lord,
bless God's holy name!
2 My soul, bless the Lord,
hold dear all God's gifts!

3 Bless God, who forgives your sin
and heals every illness,
4 who snatches you from death
and enfolds you with tender care,
5 who fills your life with richness
and gives you an eagle's strength.

◆

6 The Lord, who works justice
and defends the oppressed,
7 teaches Moses and Israel
divine ways and deeds.

8 The Lord is tender and caring,
    slow to anger, rich in love.
9 God will not accuse us long,
    nor bring our sins to trial,
10 nor exact from us in kind
    what our sins deserve.

11 As high as heaven above earth,
    so great is God's love for believers.
12 As far as east from west,
    so God removes our sins.

13 As tender as father to child,
    so gentle is God to believers.
14 The Lord knows how we are made,
    remembers we are dust.

15 Our days pass by like grass,
    our prime like a flower in bloom.
16 A wind comes, the flower goes,
    empty now its place.

17 God's love is from all ages,
    God's justice beyond all time
    for believers of each generation:
18 those who keep the covenant,
    who take care to live the law.

◆

19 The Lord reigns from heaven,
    rules over all there is.
20 Bless the Lord, you angels,

strong and quick to obey,
attending to God's word.

21 Bless the Lord, you powers,
eager to serve God's will.
22 Bless the Lord, you creatures,
everywhere under God's rule.
My soul, bless the Lord!   □

104

DELIGHT IN CREATION AND IN THE CREATOR
WHO LIMITS SEAS AND WINDS,
GOVERNS SUN AND MOON, NURTURES BIRDS AND BEASTS.

———

1 I will bless you, Lord my God!
You fill the world with awe.
You dress yourself in light,
2 in rich, majestic light.

You stretched the sky like a tent,
3 built your house beyond the rain.
You ride upon the clouds,
the wind becomes your wings,
4 the storm becomes your herald,
your servants, bolts of light.

◆

5 You made the earth solid,
   fixed it for good.
6 You made the sea a cloak,
   covering hills and all.

7 At your command
   the sea fled your thunder,
8 swept over mountains,
   down the valleys to its place.
9 You set its limits,
   never to drown the earth again.

◆

10 You feed springs that feed brooks,
   rushing down ravines,
11 water for wild beasts,
   for wild asses to drink.
12 Birds nest nearby
   and sing among the leaves.

13 You drench the hills
   with rain from high heaven.
   You nourish the earth
   with what you create.

14 You make grass grow for cattle,
   make plants grow for people,
   food to eat from the earth
15 and wine to warm the heart,

oil to glisten on faces
and bread for bodily strength.

16 In Lebanon God planted trees,
the flourishing cedar.
17 Sparrows nest in the branches,
the stork in treetops.
18 High crags for wild goats,
rock holes for badgers.

◆

19 Your moon knows when to rise,
your sun when to set.
20 Your darkness brings on night
when wild beasts prowl.
21 The young lions roar to you
in search of prey.

22 They slink off to dens
to rest at daybreak,
23 then people rise to work
until the daylight fades.

◆

24 God, how fertile your genius!
You shape each thing,
you fill the world
with what you do.

25 I watch the sea, wide and deep,
filled with fish, large and small,

26 with ships that ply their trade,
   and your own toy, Leviathan.

◆

27 All look to you for food
   when they hunger;
28 you provide it and they feed.
   You open your hand, they feast;
29 you turn away, they fear.

   You steal their breath,
   they drop back into dust.
30 Breathe into them, they rise;
   the face of the earth comes alive!

◆

31 Let God's glory endure
   and the Lord delight in creating.
32 One look from God, earth quivers;
   one touch, and mountains erupt.

33 I will sing to my God,
   make music for the Lord
   as long as I live.
34 Let my song give joy to God
   who is a joy to me.
35 Rid the world of sinners,
   rid it of evil!

   I will bless you, Lord!
   Hallelujah! □

105

---

1 Give thanks, acclaim God's name,
  tell all that the Lord has done.
2 Make music and sing
  the Lord's mighty wonders!

3 Revel in God's holy name,
  delight in seeking the Lord.
4 Look always for the power,
  for the presence of God.

5 Recount the signs and wonders,
  the just decrees of God,
6 you heirs of Abraham and Jacob,
  the chosen of the Lord.

◆

7 The Lord is our God,
  judge of all the earth,
8 who remembers his covenant
  spoken to a thousand generations:

9 the agreement with Abraham,
  the oath to Isaac,
10 the firm decree to Jacob,

psalm 105

the unending promise to Israel.
11 God said, "I give you a land,
Canaan, your inheritance."

12 They were only a few,
a small band of nomads,
13 wandering from nation to nation,
from one kingdom to another.

14 God tolerated no oppression,
rebuked kings on their account.
15 "Touch not my anointed ones,
harm not my prophets."

◆

16 God spread famine across the land
breaking the very staff of life
17 and sent a man before them,
Joseph, sold as a slave.
18 His feet were bound with shackles,
his neck with iron.
19 Yet his prophecy came true,
proved right by God's word.

20 Pharaoh released him,
the ruler of nations set him free,
21 making him master of the palace,
steward of all his goods,
22 a model for princes,
a teacher of wisdom to elders.

23 Israel journeyed to Egypt,
   Jacob to the land of Ham.
24 God's people were made fruitful,
   stronger than their foes,
25 but Egypt was made bitter,
   eager to enslave them.

26 The Lord sent his servant Moses,
   and Aaron, the chosen one,
27 to give divine and fearful signs,
   to work miracles in Egypt.

28 God sent darkness and it was dark;
   still the Egyptians resisted.
29 God turned rivers into blood,
   killing their fish.
30 Frogs crawled over the land,
   into the palace of the king.

31 Moses spoke: flies and gnats
   swarmed across the country.
32 Hail poured down,
   lightning struck the land.

33 God seared vines and fig trees,
   shattered trunks and branches.
34 Moses spoke: clouds of locusts,
   grasshoppers beyond count,
35 devoured everything green,
   the fruit of the land.

36 God struck Egypt's firstborn,
   the first fruit of their strength,
37 leading Israel forth with silver and gold;

not one among them faltered.
38 Egypt, struck with fear,
was glad to see them go.

39 A cloud shaded them by day,
a fire glowed by night.
40 Israel prayed and God sent quail,
fed them with bread from heaven,
41 opened a rock and water gushed,
streams flowed through dry land.

◆

42 Yes, God remembered his sacred word
to Abraham, his servant,
43 and brought forth his people,
the chosen ones, singing for joy.

44 The Lord gave them land
where others had toiled,
45 that they keep the commandments
and cherish the law of God.

Hallelujah! □

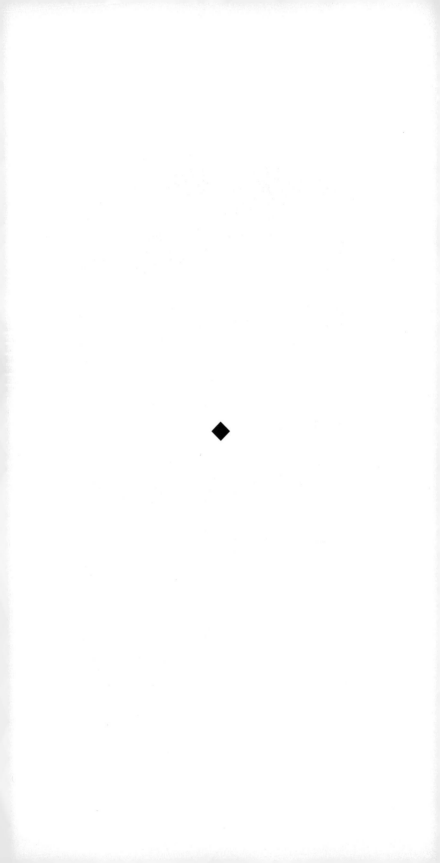

106

1 Hallelujah!

◆

Praise the Lord of goodness,
the God of lasting love.
2 Who can tell the Lord's wonders,
or sing enough praise?
3 Happy those who keep the law
and always act with justice.

4 Think of me, Lord,
when you bless your people;
share with me your salvation,
5 your blessing for your chosen ones.
Then I will rejoice with your nation
and praise you as one of your own.

◆

6 Like our ancestors we sinned,
we acted badly, wickedly.
7 While in Egypt, our ancestors
ignored your signs.

They forgot your kind deeds
and rebelled at the Reed Sea.

8 Yet God saved them,
revealed divine power,
true to his name.
9 God's rebuke cleared a dry path
through the depths of the sea,
10 freeing his people from the enemy's grip,
snatching them from hostile hands.

11 The waters swallowed their foes,
not one of them survived.
12 Then Israel trusted God's word
and sang songs of praise.

13 Quickly, they forgot his works,
ignored the divine plan.
14 In the desert they were greedy,
in the wasteland they tested the Lord.
15 He gave them what they wanted,
but let disease waste them away.
16 Their jealousy raged against Moses,
against Aaron, the Lord's holy one.

17 The earth split open to swallow Dathan,
closing over Abiram's mob.
18 Fire blazed against them,
flames devoured the wicked.
19 They fashioned a calf at Horeb,
bowed low and worshiped it.
20 They traded their God
for a grass-chewing idol.

21 They forgot God, their savior,
   the One who gave signs in Egypt,
22 marvels in the land of Pharaoh,
   and terror at the Reed Sea,
23 the One who would have destroyed them,
   had not Moses, God's chosen one,
   stood alone before him,
   deflecting the divine wrath.

24 They despised the land of promise,
   would not trust God's word.
25 They grumbled in their tents,
   refused to obey the Lord,
26 who raised a hand
   to strike them in the wilderness,
27 to scatter their descendants
   among the nations of the earth.

28 They worshiped the god of Peor
   and ate sacrifices of death.
29 They provoked the Lord with their crimes,
   and a plague stalked them down.
30 But Phinehas intervened,
   and the plague was checked.
31 This has been to his credit
   from age to age.

32 At the oasis of Meribah,
   how they angered God,
   forced Moses to suffer for them,
33 making him so bitter
   that he spoke rashly.

34 They did not slay the Canaanites
   as the Lord had ordered,
35 but mingled with them,
   adopting their customs.
36 Snared by idols,
   they bowed down,
37 sacrificing sons and daughters
   to the demons of Canaan.

38 They spilled innocent blood,
   drenching the land with guilt.
39 Their deeds polluted them,
   made them act like prostitutes.
40 Then the Lord flared with anger,
   disgusted with his people,
41 and handed them to the nations,
   to be ruled by their foes.

42 They oppressed and crushed them
   under the weight of their power.
43 Again and again God freed them,
   but they were stubborn
   and their evil brought them down.

44 The Lord saw their plight,
   heard their cry of distress,
45 and remembering his covenant,
   relented with great mercy,
46 loving them like a mother
   in the sight of their captors.

◆

47 Lord our God, save us.
   Gather us from the nations
   to give thanks to your holy name
   and rejoice in praising you.

◆　◆　◆

48 Blessed is the Lord,
   the God of Israel,
   from eternity to eternity.
   Let all the people sing
   "Amen! Hallelujah!"　☐

107

1 Give thanks to the Lord of goodness,
for God is lasting love.

2 Let those saved by God
tell their story:
how the Lord snatched them
from the oppressor's might,
3 gathering them from east and west,
from north and south.

4 They wandered through wasteland,
trekked over sands,
finding no city, no home.
5 Weak from hunger and thirst,
their lives were fading away.

6 Then they cried out to God,
who snatched them from danger,
7 leading them up a straight road
to a place they could settle.

8 Let them celebrate God's love,
all the wonders revealed to them.

psalm 107

9 The Lord slaked their thirst
   and filled their aching bellies.

◆

10 There were some confined in darkness,
   chained by suffering,
11 for they rejected God's word,
12 scorned the plan of the Most High.
   Burdened by their misery,
   they fell with no one to help.

13 Then they cried out,
   and God snatched them from danger,
14 shattering their fetters,
   banishing the darkness.

15 Let them celebrate God's love,
   all the wonders revealed to them.
16 The Lord smashed iron bars
   and doors of bronze.

◆

17 Disease struck down others
   for rebelling in their sin.
18 Sickened by food,
   they almost died.

19 Then they cried out,
   and God snatched them from danger,
20 spoke a word of healing,
   and kept them alive.

psalm 107

21 Let them celebrate God's love,
   all the wonders revealed to them.
22 Let them offer a sacrifice of praise
   and tell their story with joy.

◆

23 Sailors went down to the sea,
   traders on merchant ships,
24 and saw the works of the Lord,
   all the wonders of the deep.

25 At God's command,
   a storm whipped up the waves,
26 high as the rolling clouds,
   low as the fathomless depths.
   Seafarers trembled,
27 lurching and reeling like drunks,
   helpless without their skills.

28 Then they cried out,
   and God snatched them from danger,
29 hushing the wind,
   stilling the waters.
30 They rejoiced in the calm
   as God brought them to port.

31 Let them celebrate God's love,
   all the wonders revealed to them.
32 Let the assembly shout "Hallelujah"
   and the elders sing praise in the temple.

◆

33 God turns rivers into sand,
   springs to thirsty ground,
34 rich earth to salt flats,
   when evil dwells in a land.

35 But God turns desert to flowing water,
   dry land to fertile valleys,
36 and gives this place to the hungry
   where they build their city.

37 They sow crops, plant vines,
   and gather the harvest.
38 With God's blessing they prosper;
   people and cattle increase.

39 But if they fail to prosper
   and suffer oppression and pain,
40 God will scorn their leaders
   and make them wander in chaos.
41 But God will lift up the poor,
   shepherding them like flocks.

42 Good hearts, rejoice!
   evil mouths, be shut!
43 Let the wise listen
   and wonder at God's great love.   □

108

**GOD'S LOVE FILLS THE HEAVENS;
GOD'S STRENGTH ALONE GUARANTEES VICTORY.
PRAISE JUXTAPOSED WITH A PASSIONATE PLEA.**

---

1 A song. A psalm of David.

◆

2 I have decided, O God,
  I will sing of your glory,
  will sing your praise.
3 Awake, my harp and lyre,
  so I can wake up the dawn.

4 I will lift my voice,
  sing of you, Lord, to all nations.
5 For your love fills the heavens,
  your unfailing love, the sky.

6 O God, rise high above the heavens!
  Spread your glory across the earth!
7 Deliver those you love,
  use your strength to rescue me.

◆

8 God decreed in the temple:
  "I give away Shechem,

parcel out Succoth.
9 Manasseh and Gilead are mine.

"With Ephraim as my helmet,
and Judah my spear,
10 I will make Moab my wash bowl,
trample Edom under my feet,
and over Philistia shout in triumph."

11 Who will help me, Lord,
scale the heights of Edom
and breach the city wall?
12 God, will you keep holding back?
Will you desert our camp?

13 Stand by us against the enemy,
all other aid is worthless.
14 With you the battle is ours,
you will crush our foes.   □

109

1 For the choirmaster. A psalm of David.

◆

God of my prayer,
do not stay mute!

2 Voices are raised against me,
full of evil and deceit.
They pursue me with lies,
3 surround me with cursing,
attack for no cause.

4 I treat them with love,
but they indict me,
and yet still I pray.
5 They give back evil for good,
counter my love with hate:

6 "Appoint a crooked judge
with an accuser close by.
7 Let the verdict be guilty!
Rule even prayer a crime."

◆

8 Number the days of my accusers,
  and let others fill their office.
9 Make their children orphans,
  their spouses bereaved.

10 I want them to wander and beg,
   ruined and homeless.
11 I hope creditors take everything,
   and strangers eat up their wealth.

12 Let there be no pity,
   no one to comfort their orphans.
13 I want their line ended!
   all future names erased.

14 May God keep on record
   the crimes of father and mother,
15 and with their sins in mind
   strike their memory from the earth.

16 For my accusers know no mercy,
   they seek out the poor, the weak,
   the broken, to deal them death.

17 They loved to curse,
   let their curses recoil on them.
   They would not bless,
   let every blessing pass them by!

18 They wore their cursing like a robe;
   let it enter their bodies like water,
   stick like fat to their bones.

psalm 109

19 Let it be a robe that constricts,
   a belt that always binds.

20 So may God pay my accusers
   who murder me with lies!

◆

21 God, you are my Lord.
   Be true to your name,
   show mercy and rescue me.

22 For I am poor and weak,
   my heart is wounded;
23 I fade like a thinning shadow,
   I am brushed off like a locust.

24 Fasting makes my knees weak,
   my body skin and bones.
25 I am the object of scorn,
   they see me and shake their heads.

26 Help me, Lord my God.
   Show mercy and rescue me,
27 so they see your hand at work
   and know that you have acted.

28 Bless me, though they curse.
   Make them rise only to fall,
   and so give your servant joy!
29 Let them wear their disgrace,
   put on shame for clothing.

30 I raise my voice in thanks
  to praise God in the assembly:
31 for the Lord stands by victims,
  saves their life from judgment. □

110

**POWER IS GROUNDED IN THE COVENANT.
THE RULER WHO STANDS WITH GOD
HAS THE LOYALTY OF THE PEOPLE.**

---

1 *A psalm of David.*

The Lord decrees to the king:
"Take the throne at my right hand,
I will make your enemies a footrest.
2 I will raise your scepter
over Zion and beyond,
over all your enemies.

3 "Your people stand behind you
on the day you take command.
You are made holy, splendid,
newborn like the dawn,
fresh like the dew."

4 God's oath is firm:
"You are a priest for ever,
the rightful king by my decree."

5 The Lord stands at your side
to destroy kings
on the day of wrath.

6 God executes judgment,
crushes the heads of nations,
and brings carnage worldwide.
7 The victor drinks
from a wayside stream
and rises refreshed.   □

111

GOD IS FAITHFUL, JUST AND TRUE, MERCIFUL AND KIND.
FOR THOSE WHO FEAR GOD,
THE COVENANT IS PROTECTION AND NOURISHMENT.

1 *Hallelujah!*

With my whole heart
I praise the Lord among the just.
2 Great are God's works,
a delight to explore.
3 In splendor, in majesty,
God's justice will stand.

4 Who can forget God's wonders!
a God, merciful and kind
5 who nourished the faithful,

upheld the covenant,
6 and revealed mighty deeds,
  giving them the land of pagans.

7 Faithful, just, and true
  are all God's decrees:
8 each law in its place,
  valid for ever.

9 The Lord redeems the faithful,
  decrees a lasting covenant.
  Holy and awesome God's name!

10 Fear of the Lord is wisdom's crown,
   wise are those who live by it.
   Praise the Lord for ever! □

112

**THE PATH OF LIFE BRINGS LIFE;
THE PATH OF DEATH BRINGS DEATH.
THE UPRIGHT DELIGHT IN GOD'S LOVE.**

1 *Hallelujah!*

Happy those who love God
and delight in the law.
2 Their children shall be blest,
  strong and upright in the land.

3 Their households thrive,
   their integrity stands firm.
4 A light shines on them in darkness,
   a God of mercy and justice.

5 The good lend freely
   and deal fairly,
6 they will never stumble;
   their justice shall be remembered.

7 Bad news holds no power,
   strong hearts trust God.
8 Steady and fearless,
   they look down on their enemy.

9 They support the poor,
   their integrity stands firm,
   their strength brings them honor.

10 Hatred devours the wicked.
    They grind their teeth;
    their hopes turn to ashes.   □

113

THERE IS NO GOD ABOVE THE LORD,
NO OTHER WHO CAN BEND IN COMPASSION
TO RAISE THE WEAK FROM THE DUST.

1 Hallelujah!

Servants of God, praise,
praise the name of the Lord.
2 Bless the Lord's name
now and always.
3 Praise the Lord's name
here and in every place,
from east to west.

4 The Lord towers above nations,
God's glory shines over the heavens.
5 Who compares to our God?
Who is enthroned so high?

6 The Lord bends down
to see heaven and earth,
7 to raise the weak from the dust
and lift the poor from the mire,
8 to seat them with princes
in the company of their leaders.

9 The childless, no longer alone,
rejoice now in many children.

Hallelujah! □

psalm 113

114

AT ISRAEL'S DELIVERANCE FROM EGYPT
ALL CREATION TOOK NOTE.
WITH GOD, ALL THINGS ARE POSSIBLE.

1 Israel marches out of Egypt,
  Jacob leaves an alien people.
2 Judah becomes a holy place,
  Israel, God's domain.

3 The sea pulls back for them,
  the Jordan flees in retreat.
4 Mountains jump like rams,
  hills like lambs in fear.

5 Why shrink back, O sea?
  Jordan, why recoil?
6 Why shudder, mountains, like rams?
  Why quiver, hills, like lambs?

7 Tremble! earth, before the Lord,
  before the God of Jacob,
8 who turns rock to water,
  flint to gushing streams. □

115

1 Not to us, Lord, not to us,
  but to your name give glory,
  because of your love,
  because of your truth.

2 Why do the nations say,
  "Where is their God?"
3 Our God is in the heavens
  and answers to no one.

4 Their gods are crafted by hand,
  mere silver and gold,
5 with mouths that are mute
  and eyes that are blind,
6 with ears that are deaf
  and noses that cannot smell.

7 Their hands cannot feel,
  their feet cannot walk,
  their throats are silent.
8 Their makers, their worshipers
  will be just like them.

◆

9 Let Israel trust God,
  their help and shield.
10 Let the house of Aaron trust God,
  their help and shield.
11 Let all believers trust God,
  their help and shield.

12 The Lord has remembered us
  and will bless us,
  will bless the house of Israel,
  will bless the house of Aaron.
13 God will bless all believers,
  the small and the great.

14 May God bless you more and more,
  bless all your children.
15 May you truly be blest
  by the maker of heaven and earth.

16 To the Lord belong the heavens,
  to us the earth below!
17 The dead sing no Hallelujah,
  nor do those in the silent ground.
18 But we will bless you, Lord,
  now and for ever.

  Hallelujah!   □

116

AN EXPRESSION OF LOVING TRUST.
THE PSALMIST REMEMBERS DEATH'S GRIP
BUT RESTS SECURE IN GOD'S EMBRACE.

1 I am filled with love,
  for the Lord hears me;
2 the Lord bends to my voice
  whenever I call.

3 Death had me in its grip,
  the grave's trap was set,
  grief held me fast.
4 I cried out for God,
  "Please, Lord, rescue me!"

◆

5 Kind and faithful is the Lord,
  gentle is our God.
6 The Lord shelters the poor,
  raises me from the dust.
7 Rest once more, my heart,
  for you know the Lord's love.

8 God rescues me from death,
  wiping my tears,
  steadying my feet.
9 I walk with the Lord
  in this land of the living.

psalm 116

10 I believe, even as I say,
   "I am afflicted."
11 I believe, even though I scream,
   "Everyone lies!"

◆

12 What gift can ever repay
   God's gift to me?
13 I raise the cup of freedom
   as I call on God's name!
14 I fulfill my vows to you, Lord,
   standing before your assembly.

15 Lord, you hate to see
   your faithful ones die.
16 I beg you, Lord, hear me:
   it is I, the servant you love,
   I, the child of your servant.
   You freed me from death's grip.

17 I bring a gift of thanks,
   as I call on your name.
18 I fulfill my vows to you, Lord,
   standing before your assembly,
19 in the courts of your house,
   within the heart of Jerusalem.

   Hallelujah!   □

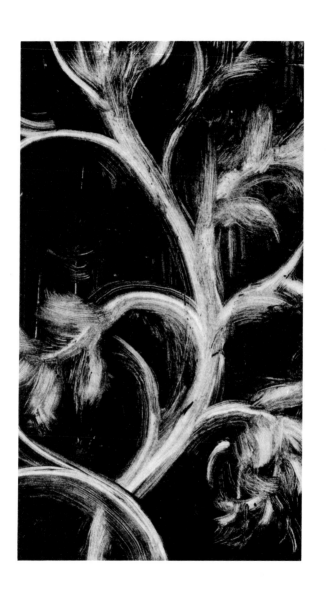

117

———

1 Praise! Give glory to God!
   Nations, peoples, give glory!

2 Strong the love embracing us.
   Faithful the Lord for ever.

   Hallelujah! □

118

———

1 Give thanks, the Lord is good,
   God's love is for ever!
2 Now let Israel say,
   "God's love is for ever!"

3 Let the house of Aaron say,
   "God's love is for ever!"

psalm 117/118

4 Let all who revere the Lord say,
  "God's love is for ever!"

◆

5 In distress I called to the Lord,
  who answered and set me free.
6 The Lord is with me, I fear not.
  What can they do to me?
7 The Lord my help is with me,
  I can face my foes.

8 Better to trust in the Lord
  than rely on human help.
9 Better to trust in the Lord
  than rely on generous hearts.

10 The nations surrounded me;
  in God's name, I will crush them!
11 Surrounded me completely;
  in God's name, I will crush them!
12 Surrounded me like bees,
  blazed like brushwood fire;
  in God's name, I will crush them!

13 I was pushed to falling,
  but the Lord gave me help.
14 My strength, my song is the Lord,
  who has become my savior.

15 Glad songs of victory sound
  within the tents of the just.

16 With right hand raised high,
   the Lord strikes with force.

17 I shall not die but live
   to tell the Lord's great deeds.
18 The Lord punished me severely,
   but did not let me die.

◆

19 Open the gates of justice,
   let me praise God within them.
20 This is the Lord's own gate,
   only the just will enter.
21 I thank you for you answered me,
   and you became my savior.

22 The stone the builders rejected
   has become the cornerstone.
23 This is the work of the Lord,
   how wonderful in our eyes.

24 This is the day the Lord made,
   let us rejoice and be glad.
25 Lord, give us the victory!
   Lord, grant us success!

26 Blest is the one who comes,
   who comes in the name of the Lord.
   We bless you from the Lord's house.
27 The Lord God is our light:
   adorn the altar with branches.

psalm 118

28 I will thank you, my God,
   I will praise you highly.
29 Give thanks, the Lord is good,
   God's love is for ever! □

119

**GOD'S LAW IS THE PATH OF TRUTH AND HOLINESS;
GOD'S SAVING WORD IS THE SOURCE OF WISDOM,
OF CONSOLATION AND DELIGHT.**

א

1 Happy the blameless,
  who keep the Lord's decrees,
2 walking the path of the law,
  seeking God with all their heart.

3 They never choose evil
  but follow God's way.
4 Lord, you charge us
  to cherish your law.

5 Steady me,
  that I may keep your commands.
6 Then, without shame,
  I can reflect on your ways.

7 I truly sing your praise,
   when I learn your justice.
8 Hold me closely,
   I shall keep your commands.

ב

9 How do the young stay pure?
   By staying close to your word!
10 I seek you with all my heart.
   Do not let me stray!

11 I cherish your word within me
   to avoid offending you.
12 I bless you, Lord,
   teach me what you require.

13 I open my mouth
   to echo your judgments.
14 I treasure your ways
   more than great riches.

15 I meditate on your laws,
   searching out your path.
16 I delight in your rules
   and remember each one.

ג

17 Be kind to me, your servant,
   that I may live your word.
18 Open my eyes
   to the beauty of your law.

psalm 119

19 Do not hide your commands
from me, a stranger.
20 Night and day, I long
to follow your teachings.

21 You rebuke those rebels
who wander from your way.
22 Save me from that shame,
for I am loyal to your rule.

23 Though princes plot against me,
still I study your decrees.
24 Your words delight me,
they are my guides.

ר

25 I slip toward death,
revive me as you promised.
26 I tell my story; you answer
and teach me your ways.

27 When you explain your laws,
I recognize your wonders.
28 I am numb with grief;
keep your word, revive me!

29 Turn me away from false paths,
bless me with your law.
30 I choose the path of truth,
cherishing your judgments.

31 I cling to your decrees,
do not shame me, Lord.

32 Eagerly I follow your path,
    for you set my heart free.

ה

33 God, teach me your ways
    and I will follow them closely.
34 Help me understand your will,
    that I may cherish your law.

35 Guide me along your path,
    a way of delight.
36 Open my heart to your laws
    and not to riches.

37 Turn my eyes from the lure of evil,
    let me live your truth.
38 Keep your promise
    to one who reveres you.

39 Spare me the shame I fear.
    How good your commands!
40 See, I want what is right,
    let your justice give me life.

ו

41 Touch me with your love, O Lord,
    save me as you promised.
42 I defy those who taunt me,
    for I trust your word.

psalm 119

43 Let me speak the whole truth,
   for I await your justice.
44 I keep your word,
   now and always.

45 I go about openly
   pursuing your law.
46 I would speak your word to kings,
   and not be ashamed.

47 For I love your ways
   and delight in following them.
48 I revere your commands
   and attend to them.

ז

49 Remember what you promised me,
   I wait in hope.
50 In sorrow, this is my comfort:
   your life-giving word.

51 The proud keep taunting me,
   still I obey your law.
52 I recall your timeless wisdom.
   How it consoles me, Lord!

53 I rage against the wicked
   who desert your law.
54 In days of exile,
   your ways are my song.

55 At night I honor your name,
   Lord, I cherish your law.

56 This is what counts for me:
   to obey your commands.

ח

57 Lord, my part
   is to keep your word.
58 I pray from my heart,
   remember your promise of mercy.

59 I consider my ways
   and return to yours.
60 I am more than eager
   to do what you command.

61 Though the wicked hem me in,
   still I remember your law.
62 Even at dead of night
   I rise to praise your justice.

63 My friends are those who revere you,
   all who keep your decrees.
64 Lord, your love fills the earth;
   teach me your laws.

ט

65 You have treated your servant well,
   just as you promised, Lord.
66 Teach me the good sense
   to put faith in your judgments.

67 I had gone astray;
   now humbled, I keep your word.
68 You give from your goodness,
   teach me how to obey.

69 I keep all your commands
   though the proud smear my name.
70 They are coldhearted,
   but I delight in your law.

71 Even suffering
   taught me your way.
72 Your law is better
   than untold wealth.

י

73 Your hands shaped me;
   inspire me to learn your wisdom.
74 The just see me and rejoice,
   because I hope in your word.

75 How right your judgments, Lord,
   how wisely you humble me.
76 Comfort me with your love,
   just as you promised.

77 Shower my life with tenderness,
   for I delight in your law.
78 Shame the proud who slander me,
   I ponder your decrees.

79 Gather your faithful ones
   to acknowledge your rule.

psalm 119

80 Keep me true to your precepts,
   free of all shame.

כ

81 All that I am longs for you,
   I wait for your word.
82 My eyes are strained from searching;
   when will you comfort me?

83 Though dried up like old leather,
   I never forget your commands.
84 How many days do I have left?
   Will you punish those who hurt me?

85 Rebels scheme to trap me,
   because they scorn your law.
86 Your commandments are true,
   my enemies are liars.

87 Help! They try to kill me,
   but I have not deserted you.
88 In your love give me life,
   so I may keep your decrees.

89 Your word is for ever, Lord,
   fixed in the heavens.
90 You made the earth firm,
   your faithfulness is eternal.

91 According to your decree
   all exist to serve you.
92 Had I not loved your law,
   I would have wasted away.

93 I never forget your word,
   for it is my life.
94 I am yours, save me!
   I study your precepts.

95 The wicked plot against me,
   but I cling to your decrees.
96 All creatures have limits,
   your rule has no frontier.

מ

97 How I love your law!
   All day it fills my thoughts.
98 I am wiser than my foes,
   your judgment is always with me.

99 I outstrip my teachers,
   for your laws have tutored me.
100 I surpass my elders,
   because I keep your precepts.

101 To follow your way
   I avoid false paths.
102 I have not spurned your judgment,
   because you are my teacher.

103 Your promises are sweet to taste,
   sweeter than honey.

104 Because your decrees give wisdom,
    I hate all evil.

נ

105 Your word is a lamp for my steps,
    a light for my path.
106 I have sworn firmly
    to uphold your just rulings.

107 I have suffered so much,
    give me the life you promise.
108 Receive, Lord, all that I say,
    and teach me your wisdom.

109 Though danger stalks,
    I will never forget your law.
110 Though the wicked set traps,
    I will not stray from you.

111 Your laws are my heritage,
    the joy of my heart for ever.
112 I am determined to obey
    for a lasting reward.

ס

113 I hate those who waver,
    but I love your law.
114 You protect and shield me,
    I trust in your word.

115 Rebels, stay away!
   I keep the commands of God.
116 Lord, uphold me and I will live,
   do not let me hope in vain.

117 Nourish me, save me,
   for your statutes are my joy.
118 You turn from those who stray,
   their thoughts are all lies.

119 You toss out the wicked like waste
   and so I cling to your laws.
120 My body trembles,
   fearing your justice.

ע

121 I live by justice and right,
   why abandon me to scoundrels?
122 Stand up for your servant,
   deliver me from the wicked.

123 My eyes seek a savior
   and look for your justice.
124 God, be merciful,
   show me your ways.

125 Help your servant understand
   and know your decrees.
126 Lord, act now!
   They break your law.

127 I love your commands
   more than finest gold.

128 I follow your precepts,
    I hate every false path.

מ

129 Wonderful are your decrees,
    I guard them with my life.
130 Unfold your word,
    enlighten the simple.

131 Longing for you,
    I thirst for your teaching.
132 Turn and favor me,
    because I love your name.

133 Let your word lead my steps,
    and evil not master me.
134 Save me from the oppressor,
    so I may keep your commands.

135 Smile upon me
    and teach me your ways.
136 I shed endless tears
    over those who break your law.

צ

137 God of justice,
    how right your judgments.
138 You establish your decrees
    in justice and truth.

139 I seethe in anger
   when enemies forget your word,
140 the promise I love,
   tested by time.

141 Discounted and shamed,
   I still remember your precepts.
142 You are eternal justice,
   your law is truth.

143 When trouble and anguish strike,
   your decrees are my joy.
144 Your commands are just,
   teach me and I will live.

ק

145 My heart begs you, Lord:
   hear me, so I can keep faith.
146 I beg you, make me free,
   so I can live your laws.

147 I face you in the cold night
   praying, waiting for your word.
148 I keep watch through the night,
   repeating what you promise.

149 Hear me, loving God,
   let your justice make me live.
150 The wicked close in on me;
   to them your law is foreign.

151 But you, Lord, are closer still,
   your law is my whole truth,

152 learned when I was young,
   fixed for all time.

ר

153 See how I suffer! Free me!
   I have not forgotten you.
154 Take my side, defend me,
   give me the life you promised.

155 No safety for the wicked:
   they spurn what you demand.
156 Lord of great mercy,
   let your word be my life.

157 Enemies hunt me down,
   yet I will not waver.
158 Traitors disgust me,
   because they break your word.

159 But I love your precepts, Lord,
   let me live in your love.
160 Truth is the heart of your word,
   every judgment stands for ever.

שׂ

161 Rulers threaten for no cause,
   I fear only your word.
162 I delight in your promise,
   it is my treasure.

163 I despise deceit
    but love your law,
164 and seven times a day
    I praise your justice.

165 Great peace with no stumbling
    for those who love your law.
166 I long for safety, Lord,
    as I follow your commandments.

167 I obey your decrees
    and revere them.
168 I keep your laws,
    for you see all that I do.

ת

169 I rejoice before you, Lord,
    let your word bring me light.
170 Hear my prayer,
    rescue me as you promised.

171 May praise be on my lips,
    because you taught me your rule.
172 May praise be on my tongue,
    because your commands are just.

173 Reach out and lead me,
    I choose your path.
174 I long to be safe, Lord,
    your law is my delight.

175 May I live to praise you,
    upheld by your word.

psalm 119

176 If I stray like a lost sheep,
　　seek out your servant,
　　for I never forget your laws.　☐

120

**THOSE WHO LOVE PEACE
FIND NO HOME AMONG THE VIOLENT;
ONLY IN GOD CAN THEY MAKE A DWELLING PLACE.**

---

1 A song of ascents.

I call out in my anguish
and God answers me.
2 Save me, Lord, from schemers,
from tongues that speak lies.

3 What will God pay you,
devious tongues?
4 Arrows sharp for battle
and white hot coals!

5 Why must I wander in Meshech,
why stay among the tents of Kedar,
6 living so long with the violent?
7 I call for peace,
they speak of war.　☐

121

**GOD IS EVER WAKEFUL AND ALWAYS NEAR,
WATCHING, SHIELDING, SHELTERING.**

1 A song of ascents.

If I look to the mountains,
will they come to my aid?
2 My help is the Lord,
who made earth and the heavens.

3 May God, ever wakeful,
keep you from stumbling;
4 the guardian of Israel
neither rests nor sleeps.

5 God shields you,
a protector by your side.
6 The sun shall not harm you by day
nor the moon at night.

7 God shelters you from evil,
securing your life.
8 God watches over you near and far,
now and always. □

122

1 A song of ascents. Of David.

With joy I heard them say,
"Let us go to the Lord's house!"
2 And now, Jerusalem,
we stand inside your gates.

3 Jerusalem, the city so built
that city and temple are one.
4 To you the tribes go up,
every tribe of the Lord.

It is the law of Israel
to honor God's name.
5 The seats of law are here,
the thrones of David's line.

6 Pray peace for Jerusalem:
happiness for your homes,
7 safety inside your walls,
peace in your great houses.

8 For love of family and friends
I say, "Peace be with you!"
9 For love of the Lord's own house
I pray for your good. □

123

1 A song of ascents.

I gaze at the heavens,
searching for you, my God.

2 A slave watches his master's hand,
a servant girl, the hand of her mistress;
so our eyes rest on you, Lord,
awaiting your kindness.

3 Have mercy, Lord, have mercy.
We have swallowed enough scorn,
4 stomached enough sneers:
the scoffing of the complacent,
the mockery of the proud. □

124

1 *A song of ascents. Of David.*

Say it, Israel!
If the Lord had not been with us,
2 if the Lord had not been for us
when enemies rose against us,
3 they would have swallowed us
in their blazing anger,
4 and the raging waters
would have swept us away—
5 rushing, surging water,
thundering over us.

6 Blessed be the Lord
for saving our flesh from their teeth,
7 for tearing the trapper's net,
so we could flutter away like birds.
8 Our help is the Lord,
creator of earth and sky. □

125

STRENGTH IS IN GOD'S EMBRACE,
BUT RULERS CAN SWAY EVEN TRUE HEARTS.
PRAY FOR GOD'S CONTINUED SUPPORT.

1 A song of ascents.

Those who trust the Lord
stand firm as Zion,
solid and strong.

2 As mountains circle Jerusalem,
Lord, you embrace your people
now and for ever.

3 Keep the rule of the wicked
far from the land of the just,
or the just may turn to evil.

4 Lord, show your goodness
to those who do good,
whose hearts are true.

5 Away with the devious,
banish them with the wicked!
Give Israel peace! □

126

---

1 A song of ascents.

The Lord brings us back to Zion,
we are like dreamers,
2 laughing, dancing,
with songs on our lips.

Other nations say,
"A new world of wonders!
The Lord is with them."
3 Yes, God works wonders.
Rejoice! Be glad!

4 Lord, bring us back
as water to thirsty land.
5 Those sowing in tears
reap, singing and laughing.

6 They left weeping, weeping,
casting the seed.
They come back singing, singing,
holding high the harvest. ☐

127

---

1 A song of ascents. Of Solomon.

If God does not build the house,
the builders work in vain.
If God does not watch over the city,
the guards watch in vain.

2 How foolish to rise early
and slave until night for bread.
Those who please God receive as much
even while they sleep.

3 Children are God's gift,
a blessing to those who bear them;
4 like arrows in the hand of an archer
are children born to the young.
5 Happy those with a full quiver:
facing their enemies at the gate,
they stand without shame! □

128

1 A song of ascents.

◆

How good to revere the Lord,
to walk in God's path.

◆

2 Your table rich from labor—
how good for you!
3 Your beloved, a fruitful vine
in the warmth of your home.

Like olive shoots,
children surround your table.
4 This is your blessing
when you revere the Lord.

◆

5 May the Lord bless you from Zion!
May you see Jerusalem prosper
every day of your life.
6 May you see your children's children,
and on Israel, peace! □

129

1 A song of ascents.

Let Israel say it:
"They often oppressed me,
2 oppressed me from my youth,
but they never crushed me."

3 They plowed into my back,
cutting deep furrows,
4 but God has proved just
and broke their wicked chains.

5 Let those who hate Zion
be ashamed and retreat!
6 Let the east wind dry them up
like weeds on a rooftop.

7 Reapers cannot cut a handful,
nor harvesters gather enough to hold.
8 No passer-by will say,
"The Lord's blessing upon you.
We bless you in God's name!" □

130

**GOD HEARS CRIES OF REPENTANCE.
THOSE WHO TRUST GOD'S WORD FIND MERCY.**

1 *A song of ascents.*

From the depths I call to you,
2 Lord, hear my cry.
Catch the sound of my voice
raised up, pleading.

3 If you record our sins,
Lord, who could survive?
4 But because you forgive
we stand in awe.

5 I trust in God's word,
I trust in the Lord.
6 More than sentries for dawn
I watch for the Lord.

More than sentries for dawn
7 let Israel watch.
The Lord will bring mercy
and grant full pardon.
8 The Lord will free Israel
from all its sins. ☐

131

1 A song of ascents.

Lord, I am not proud,
holding my head too high,
reaching beyond my grasp.

2 No, I am calm and tranquil
like a weaned child
resting in its mother's arms:
my whole being at rest.

3 Let Israel rest in the Lord,
now and for ever. ☐

132

1 A song of ascents.

◆

Lord, remember David
2 in all his humility.
He swore an oath to you,
O Mighty God of Jacob:

3 "I will not enter my home,
nor lie down on my bed.
4 I will not close my eyes
nor will I sleep
5 until I find a place for the Lord,
a house for the Mighty God of Jacob."

◆

6 We heard about it in Ephrata,
in the fields of Yaarim:
7 "Let us go to God's house,
let us worship at God's throne."

8 Lord, come to your resting place,
   you and your ark of power.
9 May your priests dress for the feast,
   and your faithful shout for joy.

10 Be loyal to David, your servant,
   do not reject your anointed.
11 You once swore to David
   and will not break your word:
   "Your child will ascend your throne.

12 "If your heirs then keep my laws,
   if they keep my covenant,
   their children will rule
   from your throne for ever."

◆

13 The Lord has chosen Zion,
   desired it as a home.
14 "This is my resting place,
   I choose to live here for ever.

15 "I will bless it with abundance,
   even the poor will have food.
16 I will vest the priests in holiness,
   and the faithful will shout for joy.

17 "Here I will strengthen David's power
   and light a lamp for my anointed.
18 His enemies I will clothe in shame,
   but on him a crown will shine." ☐

133

OIL FOR ANOINTING, DEW FOR REFRESHMENT:
THESE ARE SIGNS OF GOD'S BLESSING,
SIGNS OF ABUNDANCE, SIGNS OF HOLY LIVING.

1 A song of ascents. Of David.

How good it is, how wonderful,
wherever people live as one!

2 It is like sacred oil on the head
flowing down Aaron's beard,
down to the collar of his robe.
3 It is like the dew of Hermon
running down the mountains of Zion.

There God gives blessing:
life for ever. □

134

**HANDS LIFTED IN PRAYER
ACKNOWLEDGE DEPENDENCE ON GOD.
WITH THIS GESTURE, ALL GROUND BECOMES HOLY
AND ZION'S BLESSINGS ARE EVERYWHERE.**

1 A song of ascents.

Bless the Lord,
all who serve in God's house,
who stand watch
throughout the night.

2 Lift up your hands
in the holy place
and bless the Lord.

3 And may God,
the maker of earth and sky,
bless you from Zion. □

135

1 Hallelujah!

◆

Praise the name of the Lord,
give praise, faithful servants,
2 who stand in the courtyard,
gathered at God's house.

3 Sing hymns, for God is good.
Sing God's name, our delight,
4 for the Lord chose Jacob,
Israel as a special treasure.

5 I know the Lord is great,
surpassing every little god.
6 What God wills, God does
in heaven and earth,
in the deepest sea.

7 God blankets earth with clouds,
strikes lightning for the rain,
releases wind from the storehouse.

8 God killed Egypt's firstborn,
both humans and beasts,
9 doing wondrous signs in Egypt
against Pharoah and his aides.

10 God struck down nations,
killed mighty kings,
11 Sihon, king of the Amorites,
Og, king of Bashan,
all the kings of Canaan.

12 Then God gave Israel their land,
a gift for them to keep.
13 Your name lives for ever, Lord,
your renown never fades,
14 for you give your people justice
and attend to their needs.

◆

15 Pagan idols are silver and gold
crafted by human hands.
16 Their mouths cannot speak,
their eyes do not see.

17 Their ears hear nothing,
their nostrils do not breathe.
18 Their makers who rely on them
become like these hollow images.

psalm 135

◆

19 Bless God, house of Israel,
20 house of Aaron, house of Levi,
every faithful one.

21 Blest be the Lord of Zion,
who calls Jerusalem home.

Hallelujah!   □

136

GOD'S LASTING LOVE IS THE REFRAIN.
THIS LITANY CHANTS GOD'S SAVING ACTIONS
AND EXPRESSES GRATITUDE FOR ALL GOD'S DEEDS.

1 Our God is good, give thanks!
God's love is for ever!
2 Our God of gods, give thanks!
God's love is for ever!
3 Our Lord of lords, give thanks!
God's love is for ever!

◆

4 Alone the maker of worlds!
God's love is for ever!

psalm 136

5 Architect for the skies!
   God's love is for ever!
6 Spread land on the sea!
   God's love is for ever!

7 Set the great lights above!
   God's love is for ever!
8 The sun to rule the day!
   God's love is for ever!
9 The moon and stars, the night!
   God's love is for ever!

10 Struck down Egypt's firstborn!
   God's love is for ever!
11 Guided Israel's escape!
   God's love is for ever!
12 Held out a mighty arm!
   God's love is for ever!

13 Split in two the Reed Sea!
   God's love is for ever!
14 Led Israel across!
   God's love is for ever!
15 Drowned Pharaoh and his troops!
   God's love is for ever!

16 Led the desert trek!
   God's love is for ever!
17 Struck down mighty tribes!
   God's love is for ever!

psalm 136

18 Killed powerful kings!
God's love is for ever!

19 Sihon, the Amorite king!
God's love is for ever!
20 And Og, Bashan's king!
God's love is for ever!
21 Gave Israel a land!
God's love is for ever!
22 For God's servant to keep!
God's love is for ever!

◆

23 Remembered our distress!
God's love is for ever!
24 Kept us from defeat!
God's love is for ever!
25 God feeds all living things!
God's love is for ever!
26 God in heaven, be thanked!
God's love is for ever!   □

psalm 136

137

1 By the rivers of Babylon
we sat weeping,
remembering Zion.
2 There on the poplars
we hung our harps.

3 Our captors shouted
for happy songs,
for songs of festival.
"Sing!" they cried,
"the songs of Zion."

4 How could we sing
the song of the Lord
in a foreign land?

5 Jerusalem forgotten?
Wither my hand!
6 Jerusalem forgotten?
Silence my voice!
if I do not seek you
as my greatest joy.

◆

7 Lord, never forget
that crime of Edom
against your city,
the day they cried,
"Strip! Smash her to the ground!"

8 Doomed Babylon, be cursed!
Good for those who deal you
evil for evil!
Good for those who destroy you,
who smash your children at the walls. □

138

**GOD HEARS THE POOR, REACHES OUT.
RULERS EVERYWHERE SING PRAISE:
GOD ALONE GIVES STRENGTH AND PROTECTION.**

1 *Of David.*

I thank you with all I am,
I join heaven's chorus.
2 I bow toward your holy temple,
to praise your name.

By your love and fidelity,
you display to all
the glory of your name and promise.
3 As soon as I call, you act,
renewing my strength.

4 Around the world,
rulers praise you
for your commanding word.
5 They sing of your ways,
"Great is your glory, Lord."

6 Though high up,
you see the lowly;
though far away,
you keep an eye on the proud.

7 When I face an opponent,
you keep me alive.
You reach out your hand,
your right hand saves me.

8 Lord, take up my cause,
your love lasts for ever.
Do not abandon
what your hands have made.   □

139

1 For the choirmaster. A psalm of David.

◆

You search me, Lord, and know me.
2 Wherever I sit or stand,
you read my inmost thoughts;
3 whenever I walk or rest,
you know where I have been.

4 Before a word slips from my tongue,
Lord, you know what I will say.
5 You close in on me,
pressing your hand upon me.
6 All this overwhelms me—
too much to understand!

7 Where can I hide from you?
How can I escape your presence?
8 I scale the heavens, you are there!
I plunge to the depths, you are there!

9 If I fly toward the dawn,
or settle across the sea,
10 even there you take hold of me,
your right hand directs me.

11 If I think night will hide me
   and darkness give me cover,
12 I find darkness is not dark.
   For your night shines like day,
   darkness and light are one.

13 You created every part of me,
   knitting me in my mother's womb.
14 For such handiwork, I praise you.
   Awesome this great wonder!
   I see it so clearly!

15 You watched every bone
   taking shape in secret,
   forming in the hidden depths.
16 You saw my body grow
   according to your design.

   You recorded all my days
   before they ever began.
17 How deep are your thoughts!
   How vast their sum!
18 like countless grains of sand,
   well beyond my grasp.

◆

19 Lord, destroy the wicked,
   save me from killers.
20 They plot evil schemes,
   they blaspheme against you.

21 How I hate those who hate you!
How I detest those who defy you!
22 I hate with a deadly hate
these enemies of mine.

23 Search my heart, probe me, God!
Test and judge my thoughts.
24 Look! do I follow crooked paths?
Lead me along your ancient way. □

140

**IN THE MIDST OF VIOLENCE,
GOD IS SHELTER.
IN GOD THERE IS A HOME FOR THE OPPRESSED.**

1 *For the choirmaster. A psalm of David.*

2 Rescue me, Lord, from the wicked,
save me from the violent.
3 They spawn evil in their hearts,
starting fights every day.
4 Their tongues strike like a serpent,
their lips hide deadly venom.

5 Free me, Lord, from their evil,
save me from the violent
who plot my downfall.

6 The arrogant hide their traps
   and set their snares for me,
   tangling my path with nets.

7 But you, Lord, are my God.
   Listen! I plead with you.
8 Be the fort that saves me, Lord,
   my helmet when the battle comes.

9 Do not side with the wicked,
   do not let their plots succeed
   or they will prevail.
10 They connive to entrap me,
   let them drown in their venom!

11 Heap hot coals upon them,
   plunge them into the deep,
   never to rise again.
12 Let liars find no place to rest,
   let evil stalk the violent
   and drive them to their ruin.

13 I know how the Lord acts,
   judging for the weak,
   vindicating the poor.
14 The just honor your name,
   the innocent live in your sight.   □

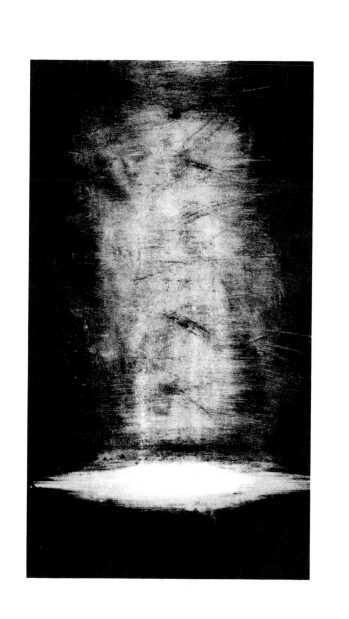

141

1 A psalm of David.

Hurry, Lord! I call and call!
Listen! I plead with you.
2 Let my prayer rise like incense,
my upraised hands,
   like an evening sacrifice.

3 Lord, guard my lips,
watch my every word.
4 Let me never speak evil
or consider hateful deeds,
let me never join the wicked
to eat their lavish meals.

5 If the just correct me,
I take their rebuke as kindness,
but the unction of the wicked
will never touch my head.
I pray and pray
against their hateful ways.

6 Let them be thrown
against a rock of judgment,
then they will know
I spoke the truth.

7 Then they will say,
  "Our bones lie broken upon the ground,
  scattered at the grave's edge."

8 Lord my God, I turn to you,
  in you I find safety.
  Do not strip me of life.
9 Do not spring on me
  the traps of the wicked.
10 Let evildoers get tangled
  in their own nets,
  but let me escape.   □

142

**I AM HUNTED DOWN, DESERTED BY FRIENDS.
WILL GOD BE ADVOCATE AND LIBERATOR?**

1 *A maskil of David.*
A prayer when he was in the cave.

2 I pray, I plead,
  I cry for mercy, Lord;
3 I pour out all my troubles,
  the story of my distress.
4 My spirit fails me.

You know the road I walk
and the traps hidden from me.
5 See what they are doing!
No one befriends me
or cares for me.

There is no escape,
6 so I turn to you, Lord.
I know you are my refuge,
all I have in the land of the living.

7 I am pleading, hear me!
I have no strength.
God, rescue me!
They hunt me down,
and overwhelm me.

8 Free me from this cage!
Then I will praise your name
and gather with the just
to thank you for your kindness. □

143

---

1 A psalm of David.

◆

Hear me, faithful Lord!
bend to my prayer,
show compassion.
2 Do not judge me harshly;
in your sight, no one is just.

◆

3 My enemy hunts me down,
grinding me to dust,
caging me with the dead
in lasting darkness.
4 My strength drains away,
my heart is numb.

5 I remember the ancient days,
I recall your wonders,
the work of your hands.
6 Dry as thirsty land,
I reach out for you.

◆

7 Answer me quickly, Lord.
My strength is spent.
Do not hide from me
or I will fall into the grave.

8 Let morning announce your love,
for it is you I trust.
Show me the right way,
I offer you myself.

9 Rescue me from my foes,
you are my only refuge, Lord.
10 Teach me your will,
for you are my God.

Graciously lead me, Lord,
on to level ground.
11 I call on your just name,
keep me safe, free from danger.

12 In your great love for me,
disarm my enemies,
destroy their power,
for I belong to you. □

144

1 Of David.

◆

Praise God, God my rock
who trains my hands for battle,
my arms for war.

2 God, my love, my safety,
my stronghold and defender,
God, my shield, my refuge,
you give me victory.

◆

3 Who are we that you care for us?
Why give a thought to mortals?
4 We are little more than breath;
our days, fleeting shadows.

5 Come, Lord, lower the heavens,
touch the mountains,
let them spew out smoke.
6 Strike lightning,

let your arrows fly,
scatter my enemies in terror.

7 Reach down from the heavens,
snatch me from crashing waves;
rescue me from strangers
8 who speak lies
and then swear to them.

◆

9 I sing you a new song, Lord,
I play my ten-stringed harp,
10 for you give victory to kings,
you rescue your servant, David.

11 Save me from the bitter sword,
deliver me from strangers,
who speak lies
and then swear to them.

◆

12 God, you shape our sons
like tall, sturdy plants;
you sculpt our daughters
like pillars for a palace.

13 You fill our barns
with all kinds of food,
you bless our fields
with sheep by the thousands
14 and fatten all our cattle.

psalm 144

There is no breach in the walls,
no outcry in the streets, no exile.
15 We are a people blest with these gifts,
blest with the Lord as our God! □

145

**PRAISE AND BLESSINGS
TO THE LORD OF ALL CREATION,
WHO IS GRACIOUS AND MERCIFUL,
FAITHFUL AND JUST, LOVING IN EVERY WAY.**

———

1 *Praise. Of David.*

I will exalt you, God my king,
for ever bless your name.
2 I will bless you every day,
for ever praise your name.

3 Great is the Lord, highly to be praised,
great beyond our reach.

4 Age to age proclaims your works,
recounts your mighty deeds.
5 I ponder your splendor and glory
and all your wonderful works.

6 They reveal your fearful power,
I tell of your great deeds.

7 They recall your ample goodness,
   joyfully sing your justice.

8 Gracious and merciful is the Lord,
   slow to anger, full of love.
9 The Lord is good in every way,
   merciful to every creature.

10 Let your works praise you, Lord,
   your faithful ones bless you.
11 Let them proclaim your glorious reign,
   let them tell of your might.

12 Let them make known to all
   your might and glorious reign.
13 Your dominion lasts for ever,
   your rule for all generations!

   The Lord is faithful in every word
   and gracious in every work.
14 The Lord supports the fallen,
   raises those bowed down.

15 The eyes of all look to you,
   you give them food in due time.
16 You open wide your hand
   to feed all living things.

17 The Lord is just in every way,
   loving in every deed.
18 The Lord is near to those who call,
   who cry out from their hearts.

19 God grants them their desires,
   hears their cry and saves them.

psalm 145

20 Those who love God are kept alive;
the wicked, the Lord destroys.

21 I will sing the Lord's praise,
all flesh will bless God's Name,
holy, both now and for ever.   □

146

**GOD ALONE IS WORTHY OF TRUST.
GOD ALONE IS FAITHFUL AND COMPASSIONATE.
GOD ALONE REIGNS FOREVER.**

1 *Hallelujah!*

Praise the Lord, my heart!
2 My whole life, give praise.
Let me sing to God
as long as I live.

3 Never depend on rulers:
born of earth, they cannot save.
4 They die, they turn to dust.
That day, their plans crumble.

5 They are wise who depend on God,
who look to Jacob's Lord,
6 creator of heaven and earth,
maker of the teeming sea.

The Lord keeps faith for ever,
7 giving food to the hungry,
justice to the poor,
freedom to captives.

8 The Lord opens blind eyes
and straightens the bent,
comforting widows and orphans,
9 protecting the stranger.
The Lord loves the just
but blocks the path of the wicked.

10 Zion, praise the Lord!
Your God reigns for ever,
from generation to generation.
Hallelujah! □

147

**GOD SPEAKS THE CREATIVE WORD.
GOD'S WORD IS WISDOM; GOD'S WORD IS LIFE.**

1 *Hallelujah!*

◆

How good to sing God praise!
How lovely the sound!

2 The Lord rebuilds Jerusalem
   and gathers the exiles of Israel,
3 healing the brokenhearted,
   binding their aching wounds.

4 God fixes the number of stars,
   calling each by name.
5 Great is our God and powerful,
   wise beyond all telling.
6 The Lord upholds the poor
   but lets the wicked fall.

7 Sing thanks to the Lord,
   sound the harp for our God.
8 The Lord stretches the clouds,
   sending rain to the earth,
   clothing mountains with green.

9 The Lord feeds the cattle
   and young ravens when they call.
10 A horse's strength, a runner's speed—
   they count for nothing!
11 The Lord favors the reverent,
   those who trust in God's mercy.

12 Jerusalem, give glory!
   Praise God with song, O Zion!
13 For the Lord strengthens your gates

guarding your children within.
14 The Lord fills your land with peace,
   giving you golden wheat.

15 God speaks to the earth,
   the word speeds forth.
16 The Lord sends heavy snow
   and scatters frost like ashes.

17 The Lord hurls chunks of hail.
   Who can stand such cold?
18 God speaks, the ice melts;
   God breathes, the streams flow.

19 God speaks his word to Jacob,
   to Israel, his laws and decrees.
20 God has not done this for others,
   no others receive this wisdom.

Hallelujah! □

148

1 Hallelujah!

◆

Praise the Lord!
Across the heavens,
from the heights,
2 all you angels, heavenly beings,
sing praise, sing praise!

3 Sun and moon, glittering stars,
sing praise, sing praise.
4 Highest heavens, rain clouds,
sing praise, sing praise.

5 Praise God's name,
whose word called you forth
6 and fixed you in place for ever
by eternal decree.

◆

7 Let there be praise:
   from depths of the earth,
   from creatures of the deep.

8 Fire and hail, snow and mist,
   storms, winds,
9 mountains, hills,
   fruit trees and cedars,
10 wild beasts and tame,
   snakes and birds,

11 princes, judges,
   rulers, subjects,
12 men, women,
   old and young,
13 praise, praise the holy name,
   this name beyond all names.

   God's splendor above the earth,
   above the heavens,
14 gives strength to the nation,
   glory to the faithful,
   a people close to the Lord.
   Israel, let there be praise!   □

psalm 148

149

1 Hallelujah!

Sing a new song, you faithful,
praise God in the assembly.
2 Israel, rejoice in your maker,
Zion, in your king.
3 Dance in the Lord's name,
sounding harp and tambourine.

4 The Lord delights
in saving a helpless people.
5 Revel in God's glory,
join in clan by clan.
6 Shout praise from your throat,
sword flashing in hand

7 to discipline nations
and punish the wicked,
8 to shackle their kings
and chain their leaders,
9 and execute God's sentence.
You faithful, this is your glory!

Hallelujah!   □

150

1 Hallelujah!

Praise! Praise God in the temple,
in the highest heavens!
2 Praise! Praise God's mighty deeds
and noble majesty.

3 Praise! Praise God with trumpet blasts,
with lute and harp.
4 Praise! Praise God with timbrel and dance,
with strings and pipes.

5 Praise! Praise God with crashing cymbals,
with ringing cymbals.
6 All that is alive, praise. Praise the Lord.
Hallelujah! ☐

THE BOOK OF PSALMS
Carroll Stuhlmueller, CP

Opening the Book of Psalms is like walking into a home, lived in for many generations. Photos and mementos, some ancient and some new, blend together. Some are well preserved, others were dropped and cracked by the children, still others have faded, and a few are even difficult to identify. Only the grandparents know the story of each precious remembrance—if only they were still with us.

We turn to our ancestors in the faith to hear what they tell us about this sacred home, their house of prayer, the Book of Psalms. As in the family homestead, some psalms are carefully preserved, like Psalm 70, and others are almost indecipherable, like Psalms 2:1–12 and 141:5–7. Still others, like Psalm 139, use rare Hebrew forms, possibly some Aramaic words or endings. Yet whatever the problem, this psalm is well loved. Another section of psalms, sometimes called the curse or vindictive psalms, for instance Psalm 69:23–29, may be translated confidently enough, but their angry outbursts against the enemy embarrass Jews and Christians alike and have been dropped from the liturgical prayer of most churches. The family home unfortunately still harbors its grudges and feuds. The psalms, like the home, lead us through many stages of life, necessary to carry on, even if not our finest moments.

The psalms remained so precious that the early Christians never added their own book of prayer to the New Testament. They kept with the prayer book of their religious ancestors.

FROM OBEDIENCE TO EXULTATION

In paging through our Bible we notice that this house of prayer or Book of Psalms is divided into five rooms or sections. Each of the first four rooms, or "books" as they are called, ends with a doxology of praise, differing only in the degree of excitement:

Blessed be the Lord,
God of Israel for ever.
Amen! Amen! (41:14)

Blessed be Israel's God,
Lord of wonderful deeds!
Bless God's name for ever!
Let God's glory fill the world!
Amen and Amen! (72:18–19)

Blessed be God for ever. Amen. Amen. (89:53)

Blest is the Lord,
the God of Israel,
from eternity to eternity.
Let all the people sing
"Amen! Hallelujah!" (106:48)

The first book begins with a reflection upon the law, the happy and fruitful life of the obedient person, "like a tree planted by a stream, . . . its yield always plenty," and the dismal, barren life of the wicked, "like chaff . . . blown by the wind." The fifth book concludes with Psalm 150 and its thunderous roll of hallelujahs. Thirteen variations of this Hebrew word summon every person to "praise God." The five books of psalms continuously reach to the heavens ecstatic with wonder. Whatever be the circumstances of sorrow and death, puzzlement and questioning, gratitude and confidence, joy and excitement, even anger and feelings of revenge, within the five rooms or books of psalms, each moment asks for obedience to God and ends with its Amen! Hallelujah! praising God.

THE FIVE ROOMS OF ISRAEL'S HOUSE OF PRAYER

As happens when children are born within a family, Israel was adding new rooms or "books" to its home. Each new generation faced new life situations. In many ways each of the five books holds a mirror to the age when a scribe or editor gathered its psalms together and responded to life's realities.

Dark clouds hang over the *first book* (Psalms 1–41) with a heavy presence of lament and supplication. Praise, as in Psalms 8, 19 or 29, at times interrupts the dismal landscape. Yet the majority of these psalms reflects depression days. They accompany the tears and groans of individual Jewish people after their return to a devastated homeland around 537 BCE. Despite it all, the first book ends with its Amen, its strong affirmation of faith in God's presence through it all.

Later, after the rebuilding of the Temple and its dedication in 515 BCE, another scribe, from a guild of writers under the patronage of Korah, adds a new collection of psalms. These focus on worship in the Jerusalem Temple and become the *second book*, Psalms 42–72. The signature of Korah is delicacy, longing and joyful memories of worship:

> *As a deer craves running water,*
> *I thirst for you, my God . . .*
> *I cry my heart out,*
> *I remember better days. (42:2, 5)*

The *third book* (Psalms 73–89) opens with songs, strong and confident, realistic and responsive, from a different group of writers under the name of Asaph. They seem to echo the time of the great religious reforms of Ezra around 428 BCE (see Ezra, chapter 10, and Nehemiah, chapters 8–9 and 13).

As will happen with any home, the family adds other things— a ramp for a sick or elderly person, some toys for a child, and mementos from an anniversary celebration. The *fourth book* (Psalms 90–106) collects these stray pieces.

Finally the *fifth and final book* (Psalms 107–150) contains psalms for pilgrimage to Jerusalem (Psalms 120–134), others for singing at the three great pilgrimage festivals (Psalms 113–118). Perhaps we can place this collection after the conquests of Alexander the Great, sometime around 300 BCE.

The psalms, therefore, appear as a liturgical or prayerful response to the needs of each new age of Israel's history. The scribes or editors assembled and wrote down these hymns and prayers within a book of psalms, not in any chronological order of composition but pastorally as the people needed them.

Some of this explanation depends upon the "titles" of the psalms, omitted in our liturgy but printed in our Bibles at the beginning of most of the psalms. Other aspects derive from our effort to coordinate the dominant attitude within each book of psalms with important moments in the history of Israel after the Babylonian exile.

THE WEAR AND TEAR OF USE

New generations will do more than add rooms. They shift furniture around and give old pieces new uses. A careful reading shows that the biblical Book of Psalms demonstrates the wear and tear of long use in the temple, synagogue and home. Psalm 14 repeats itself as Psalm 53; Psalm 70 appears within 40:14–18. The differences almost slip by unnoticed. While Psalms 14 and 40 address God by the divine name, Psalms 53 and 70 try to avoid that most sacred word, whose Hebrew form was never spoken in postexilic Israel except once a year by the High Priest on the feast of Yom Kippur, the Day of Atonement. In fact, "Lord" almost never occurs within one series of psalms, 42–53.

We have no certain explanation for this change from "Lord" to "God," except to suggest that the title "Lord" was too sacred for daily prayer and so its easy use struck people as offensive or blasphemous. This change in biblical times might support other changes within modern translations of the psalms. Some versions, like the one within this book, avoid words that are offensive or give a wrong meaning, like the word "men" when we really mean "women and men." The ancient Bible, especially the psalms, was primarily a liturgical text and lived within the changing circumstances of people's lives.

Still other adaptations occurred as Jewish people prayed the psalms. They composed a new Psalm 108 out of sections from two earlier psalms. How this new composition came into existence gives an excellent example of adapting earlier inspired psalms to a new situation.

Psalm 57 lays bare the fears of a timid person, hounded by people whose "teeth [are] like spears and arrows, [whose] tongues [are] sharp as swords" (verse 5). God rewards such humble patience, and the psalmist wakes the dawn to sing with harp and lyre (verse 9). Psalm 60, on the contrary, shouts defiance at the enemy and then calls upon God to "stretch out your hand, rescue us," you who "shook the land" until it "shuddered and split." In deleting parts of each psalm and combining other sections, the new Psalm 108 modifies the fierceness of Psalm 60 and strengthens the timidity of Psalm 57.

There are times today when some biblical texts and psalms are either too strident and confident, or else too weak and indecisive. We need to follow the lead of our ancestors by adapting the text, blending passages and so reaching a new message.

These matters may seem trivial, yet sometimes the character of a person or of a family home shows up in attention to small, delicate details, adapting to guests and to unexpected turns of events.

Yet changes were not made on a whim. The scribes carefully guarded the text of the psalms. By counting every letter and verse, they could determine the middle letter and the middle verse of the entire psalter. The middle letter turned out to be *ayin* within the phrase "wild boars," literally "beasts from the forest," in Psalm 80:14. This letter they elevate and so high-light in every Hebrew Bible. *Ayin* is not only a letter of the alphabet but is also the word for "eye" and "spring." Each flows with water or tears. The meaning can be: At the center of the entire psalter, the eye of God looks upon us at every moment, at times even to drop a tear of compassion.

This spirit of divine compassion is again clear in the middle *verse* of all 150 psalms:

> *Yet God, in compassion,*
> *did not destroy them,*
> *but held back anger,*
> *restrained fury,*
> *forgave their sin. (78:38)*

Wear and tear bring tears of suffering and of joy, but most of all they deepen our compassion and enable our hearts to for-give as God does.

FROM PRAISE AND DESOLATION
TO THANKSGIVING AND WISDOM

Up until now we have examined the Book (or Five Books) of Psalms as found in our Bible. The format shows a sensitivity to the changing pastoral needs of ancient Israel and directs us likewise to be sensitive to the religious and social expectations of our day and age. We turn to individual types of prayers within the psalms.

Some of the most ancient psalms are *hymns of praise*. Numbered among these are Psalms 8, 19, 29 and 104. These hymns of praise hardly, if ever, speak of sin or sorrow. Rather, with their good eye they see a presence of God that is won-drous, overwhelming and most pure. They perceive the world and humankind as good and beautiful, fresh from the cre-ative, caring hand of God:

Lord our God,
the whole world tells
the greatness of your name.
Your glory reaches
beyond the stars . . .
What is humankind
that you remember them,
the human race
that you care for them?
You treat them like gods,
dressing them in glory and splendor. (8:2, 5–6)

These hymns draw their motivation not just from God's marvelous universe but also from God's magnificent care for Israel, especially in the wilderness during the days of Moses and Miriam. Psalm 114 is the song of passover exultation:

Israel marches out of Egypt . . .
The sea pulls back for them,
the Jordan flees in retreat.
Mountains jump like rams,
hills like lambs in fear . . .
Why shudder, mountains, like rams?
Why quiver, hills, like lambs?
Tremble! earth, before the Lord,
before the God of Jacob,
who turns rock to water,
flint to gushing streams. (114:1, 3–4, 6–8)

Such hymns of praise rebound triumphantly from the majestic walls of Jerusalem's Temple. Other hymns acclaim this home of Israel's fearful yet compassionate, distant yet ever present God:

Holy mountain, beautiful height,
crown of the earth!
Zion, highest of sacred peaks,
city of the Great King!

> *God enthroned in its palaces*
> *becomes our sure defense! (48:2–4)*

Another series of early psalms provides a ritual for the enthronement of a king as well as for royal marriages and regal festivals (Psalms 2, 45, 72, 110), or as in Psalm 89, they add a prayer of supplication after a serious defeat.

Psalms of sorrow and supplication, as already mentioned, occupy major space in the first book of the psalter (Psalms 1–41). Yet these were written later than many of the hymns and show the strong influence of the prophets, especially Jeremiah, who repeatedly questioned and argued against God (see Jeremiah 12:1–5; 20:7–18). The clearest quality of this new set of psalms is honesty, even to the point of testing the limits of orthodoxy.

> *God, my God,*
> *why have you abandoned me—*
> *far from my cry, my words of pain?*
> *I call by day, you do not answer;*
> *I call by night, but find no rest. (22:1–2)*

In this psalm a person's question to God, now a part of the Bible, becomes the inspired word of God and paradoxically God's answer to the questioner. God's word is not always in crystal statements of truth. Rather, God appears within the human process of struggling without finding, of being left only with a question, bleakly and darkly in Psalm 88. The psalms embrace an absent God, mystically present in our questions.

The prayers of supplication sometimes speak in the singular, as in Psalm 22; others, voicing the community's pain and desolation, speak in the plural, as in Psalm 44. This psalm begins with an energetic statement of faith in the ancestral traditions (verses 2–9), then proceeds at once to contradict itself:

> *You, God, rescued us from danger*
> *and put our foes to shame . . .*

You force us to retreat
while the enemy plunders our goods . . .
I turn red with shame
when I hear cruel taunts
from foes wanting revenge. (44:8, 11, 16–17)

The psalm is audacious enough—or is it better to say, honest enough?—to fling the gauntlet before the deity:

Wake up! Why do you sleep, Lord? (44:24)

and so contradicts another psalm which quietly and confidently addresses "the guardian of Israel [who] neither rests nor sleeps" (Psalm 121:4). Desperately Psalm 44 plunges beyond the limits of orthodoxy, not to deny the truth but to declare that some human experiences defy all rational explanation, even that of good theologians and inspired biblical authors.

Another group of psalms, of *thanksgiving* and *confidence,* usher up front what remains only a conclusion in other psalms. Only Psalm 88 remains dark and abandoned throughout. Psalm 118 first thanks God for personal favors and then joins these with the gratitude of all Israel. Psalm 16, despite ridicule and shame heaped upon the devout Israelite, expresses a staunch, humble loyalty to God:

Lord, you measure out my portion,
the shape of my future;
you mark off the best place for me. (16:5–6)

While most of the preceding psalms spring into life from heroic moments, whether of overwhelming joy and ecstatic wonder or of deadening desolation and shameful rejection, there are still other psalms for the moderate, normal everydays of life. It is ordinarily true, as Psalm 1 states:

The Lord marks the way of the upright,
but the corrupt walk to ruin. (1:6)

This golden rule of moderation and trust is put as plainly as possible in another *psalm of the wisdom tradition:*

> *From my youth to my old age*
> *never have I seen the just cast off*
> *or their children begging bread. (37:25)*

Yet even the wisdom tradition was tested beyond its resources of correct and just retribution on earth, so that the psalmists sometimes rushed on where angels stand in fear. Wisdom psalms that seem the most down to earth, practical to the point of being pragmatic, reach the limits of earthly reward and punishment and momentarily peer into a life beyond this life. The language is not as clear as the theologian would like it to be, but it smacks of the honesty and hesitation that seem to stalk our thoughts of heaven as we pick our way over sticky quagmires of distress:

> *You teach me wisdom,*
> *leading me to glory.*
> *What more would I have in heaven?*
> *Who else delights me on earth?*
> *If mind and body fail,*
> *you, God, are my rock,*
> *my support for ever. (73:24–26)*

The longest psalm of all plods slowly, surely, faithfully over the way of each person's life, submitting each step to God's help and guidance. Psalm 119 leaves no stage of our existence without God's strong protection.

<h3 style="text-align:center">CONCLUSION</h3>

The psalms bring us home to God, no matter how we are dressed, how we feel, what we have done or left undone. What they ask is already present in our heart from the opening Psalm 1, the gift of faith in God's loving presence, to Psalm 150 with its chorus of hallelujahs. The psalms lead us through the sections or rooms of our life, always ending with a strong Amen. Walking along, we are never alone but in the company of our ancestors. When our questions arise, as happened to the two persons on their way to Emmaus, Jesus appears to declare that "everything written about me in the law of Moses and in the prophets and *psalms* must be fulfilled" (Luke 24:44). Through the psalms Jesus opens our mind to the hidden mysteries within our lives.

AFTERWORD

The idea for this liturgical psalter project was initiated in 1964 when the International Commission on English in the Liturgy (ICEL) received its mandate approved by English-speaking conferences of bishops. Among the principal charges given to ICEL in that mandate was the provision of biblical texts used in the liturgy. ICEL's first response to this aspect of its mandate was the issuance in 1967 of "English for the Mass: Part II," which contained a translation of four psalms (Psalms 25, 34, 85 and 130) and guidelines for the preparation of a liturgical psalter.

In "English for the Mass: Part II" it was explained that ICEL would undertake this project because of the special need for a text for singing. The book also listed principles that would guide the work as it developed in later years:

(1) The best existing versions both critical and literary should be consulted.

(2) Greater freedom should be allowed in translating psalms than most books of the Bible because they are poetry and must be such in English and because they are meant for the frequent and inspiring use of the people, choirs, and cantors in the liturgy.

(3) Rhythm suited to the English language should be used in the translation.

The need to provide countless vernacular texts of the various rites in a short period of time delayed the beginning of this project for another decade. Other modern English Bible translations were readily available; and the episcopal conferences of English-speaking countries authorized the psalter of one or more of these for liturgical use in their regions. The Book of Psalms from *The Jerusalem Bible, The New American Bible, The Revised Standard Version,* and also the Grail translation of the psalms provided the texts which have been used in the liturgy of the hours and for the responsorial psalm in the liturgy of the word for the past 25 or 30 years. In 1978 ICEL's Advisory Committee (the general steering committee for all ICEL projects) received authorization from the Episcopal Board

(ICEL's chief governing body made up of a bishop-representative from the 11 English-speaking member conferences of bishops) to establish a subcommittee on the liturgical psalter. Initially this subcommittee was asked to produce a statement of purposes and procedures and to provide a translation of ten psalms, representative of the various genres of psalms contained in the Book of Psalms. The members of the subcommittee included specialists in Hebrew language and poetry, liturgical history and theology, music, English poetry, and literary and language theory. Together they wrote an initial 15-page "Brief," and then undertook the translation of the first group of ten psalms. Literal and base translations were produced by the Hebraists and, in dialogue with the poets, liturgists, literary critics and musicians of the team, the texts were continually refined. In late 1981 a consultation booklet was printed which included the translation of ten psalms, their musical settings, liturgical comments on their use, explanatory textual notes and a questionnaire. This was sent to a wide variety of liturgical communities and professionals for comment and evaluation after trial use during the Easter season of 1982.

During this first limited consultation, the translation team continued its work on another set of texts, taking into account responses to the questionnaire as they became available. By Easter 1984 a larger set of 22 psalms (those most often used in the liturgy) were sent out for more extensive consultation to two thousand worship commissions, parishes, religious communities and schools in the English-speaking world. On the basis of the positive responses received in these two consultations the Episcopal Board in 1986 asked for immediate wider circulation of the psalms already completed. In 1987, 23 psalms were published, under the title *Psalms for All Seasons: From the ICEL Liturgical Psalter Project,* by the Pastoral Press in Washington D.C. The Episcopal Board at that time also authorized the completion of the full project.

To facilitate the translation of the remaining psalms and canticles according to the principles outlined in the Brief, four working groups were organized (in London, New York, Chicago, and Washington D.C.). Each group was composed of five members who possessed the various specialties necessary for the scope of the project. When a working group judged that the texts it was assigned were in presentable form, they were circulated to colleagues in each of the three other working groups for their review and written comments. This material was sent to a five-person Editorial Committee constituted from among the members of the working groups. The committee would review the comments and make any changes in the texts deemed necessary. The Editorial Committee would then circulate these next-to-final draft texts to the ICEL Advisory Committee for its review, comments, and approval. The Editorial Committee would then arrive at a final draft text on the basis of these comments.

The aims of those who have worked on this project were to create a translation (1) that would faithfully render into English the best critical Hebrew and Greek texts available; (2) that would be guided by the liturgical use of the psalms and canticles, and be fitting for musical setting; (3) that would be received by the reader or auditor as idiomatic English in contemporary poetic style; and (4) that would be sensitive to evolving gender usage in English, for example, as described in the "Criteria for the Evaluation of Inclusive Language Translations of Scriptural Texts Proposed for Liturgical Use" of the National Conference of Catholic Bishops of the United States.

I. FAITHFUL RENDERING

To assure the accuracy and integrity of the new translation, the translators have worked at all stages of the process from the Masoretic text (Biblia Hebraica Stuttgartensia). In those frequent cases where the Masoretic text is not certain or clear in meaning, significant help was provided by the witness of ancient translations (for example, the Septuagint and Vulgate), and by the expanded vocabulary and stylistic usages found in ancient nonbiblical documents of the Semitic language area.

Because this translation is intended for contemporary liturgical use, it follows the principles of dynamic equivalence, rather than formal equivalence. As any serious effort at translation, it seeks: to render accurately the meaning of the original, to convey the spirit and nuances of the original, to make complete sense in idiomatic English and achieve a certain literary quality, and, as far as possible, to produce the same effect in modern readers as the original Hebrew produced in its audience. The key to a dynamic equivalence translation, however, is a more acute awareness that a modern receptor language expresses the thought, nuances, and presuppositions of its society in modes that are often different from those of ancient societies. Thus, while a formally equivalent translation seeks to render closely the distinctive structural and semantic characteristics of the source language (for example, grammatical and rhetorical constructions, word order, tense, number and gender markers, literal translation of idioms not found in the receptor language), a dynamically equivalent translation seeks parallel structural, semantic and idiomatic units that are native to the receptor language. Indeed, to communicate as closely as possible the very content of the psalm or canticle to an English-speaking audience, ancient rhetorical structures and grammatical forms must be adapted to English modes of expression.

Particular mention must be made of a central characteristic of the Hebrew text of the psalms that does not have a direct parallel in English: namely, the use of the Tetragrammaton (YHWH) as the unvoiced Hebrew name for God. Out of respect for the traditional Jewish reverence for this name, it is not used in this translation. Instead, following current scholarly understanding of the divine name(s), "God" and "Lord" are used somewhat interchangeably to translate "YHWH", "adonay", and "elohim". In the Hebrew Scriptures "God" and "Lord" are often used as parallel terms (Exodus 15:17; Deuteronomy 7:9; 2 Kings 19:4; Isaiah 3:17; Psalms 7:9–10; 35:22; 71:5). Different stages of development of the Scriptures also show different practices in the use of the divine name, as does the practice of the Greek translators of the Septuagint who offered varied renderings. For example, Hebrew "YHWH" is translated as "theos" in Septuagint Genesis 4:16; 6:7, and in Psalm 70 (71):1; while Hebrew "elohim" is translated as "kurios" in Septuagint Genesis 21:2, 6; 48:15; and Psalm 76 (77):2.

The choice of "Lord" and "God" in this translation is influenced by this tradition, as well as by considerations central to this project: the principles of a dynamically equivalent translation, of modern English style noted for its compression of language, and of poetry with its attention to poetic rhythm, repetition and/or variation.

II. A LITURGICAL TRANSLATION
FOR MUSICAL ACCOMPANIMENT

This translation takes into account the original liturgical contexts of these works (e.g. lament, thanksgiving, wisdom, enthronement psalms), as well as their traditional use in Christian worship.

Because these texts are essentially liturgical works, their translation presumes musical performance as the norm, though they would also be suitable for choral recitation and private devotion. Special care is given to the sounds of words, their sequence and rhythm, as well as to their sense, not only for poetic purposes but also that they might be attractive to composers and musicians.

Decisions as to the division of strophes, use of refrains, syllabic count and distribution of stresses within a line were made according to the nature of the text under consideration, its use in the liturgy, and the poetic judgment of the translating group. A certain regularity of stress pattern was sought as desirable

but was not slavishly applied. More than two unstressed syllables between stressed syllables were avoided wherever possible,
as were lame cadences. Stressed final syllables were preferred
at endline, and diphthongs were avoided. Care was also taken
to facilitate singing by rejecting words and word sequences
with consonantal clusters difficult to articulate.

III. TRANSLATION INTO CONTEMPORARY
ENGLISH POETIC STYLE

Keeping to the principle of dynamic equivalence, this translation seeks to render the psalms and canticles in a style that
is idiomatically English and in a contemporary poetic form
marked by heightened imagery and concision. The translators
sought a balance between a vernacular language that would be
immediately communicative and a poetic liturgical language
that would draw people out of their familiar worlds and eluci-
date their ordinary experience.

Toward this end efforts are made in this translation to bring
to the surface metaphors that are submerged in the original
language and in other translations. The attempt is made to
render these metaphors with the same immediacy and con-
creteness they possessed in the original. The vocabulary exhibits
a strong preference for monosyllables and Anglo-Saxon root
words, rather than words of Latinate origin. The liveliness
of the Hebrew texts is conveyed through the use of a wider
variety of striking concrete verbs than is found in other translations. These often serve as the vehicle for the metaphors and
imagery, and their energy is preserved by being frequently in
the present tense.

A well-known structural component of Hebrew poetry is the
use of parallelism in its various forms: synonymous, antithet-
ical or synthetic (in which there is no strict parallel as such, but
rather a close connection of logic or consequence or addition).
Most psalms employ the last type and thus cannot be said to
employ simply two matching expressions that reiterate the

same thought. Translators thus need to recognize several possible levels of meaning in Hebrew couplets and not think that a merely mechanical reproduction of paired lines always represents an adequate rendering of the text. Furthermore, though the occasional use of parallelism and other rhetorical figures are certainly not foreign to modern poetry, a consistent use of such figures would strike a contemporary reader with the stateliness, but also the remoteness and stasis of the Augustan verse of the eighteenth century.

To achieve a more contemporary poetic style, this translation employs a number of strategies to deal with parallelisms: first, word order is sometimes changed, and the second subject is absorbed into the first or replaced by a pronoun. Thus, the strictly parallel form A:B:C::A:B:C might appear as A:B:C::B:C or A:B:C::(a):B:C, as in Psalm 72:9:

> Literal Hebrew:
> *Before him shall bow down the siyyim (meaning unclear)*
> *And his enemies the dust will lick.*

> ICEL translation:
> *Enemies will cower before him,*
> *they will lick the dust.*

Second, enjambment is used to run the thought of two parallel lines into a continuous sentence, as in Psalm 47:6:

> Literal Hebrew:
> *God goes up to shouts of praise;*
> *the Lord to the sound of the trumpet.*

> ICEL translation:
> *God ascends the mountain*
> *to cheers and trumpet blasts.*

> *(Note that "mountain" is added here for the sake of clarity for a modern audience who might otherwise think God is ascending to the heavens rather than to the temple on Mount Zion.)*

Through all these various means, this translation hopes to render the psalms and canticles in a contemporary English poetic and liturgical style that is in the spirit of the direction given by the Holy See's 1969 Instruction on the Translation of Liturgical Texts:

> *The prayer of the church is always the prayer of some actual community, assembled here and now. It is not sufficient that a formula handed down from some other time or region be translated verbatim, even if accurately, for liturgical use. The formula translated must become the genuine prayer of the congregation and in it each of its members should be able to find and express himself or herself (no. 20).*

IV. INCLUSIVE LANGUAGE

One of the most notable characteristics of contemporary English-speaking communities is a growing sensitivity to gender-exclusive language. The psalms, in particular, reflect the prayer of the temple liturgy that was voiced by an allmale assembly; their expression consequently is influenced by the experience, imaginative vision and language of their originating congregation. Even so, this cultic perspective conceals the memory recorded elsewhere in the Old Testament of the women of Israel as faithful devotees, songwriters, and leaders of song for the covenant community: e.g., Miriam (Exodus 15:20–21), Hannah (1 Samuel 2:1–10), and Judith (Judith 16:1–17). Surely a liturgical psalter that is to serve the living faith of a covenant community manifestly composed of men and women ought neither impede nor distort the good news of God's all-inclusive embrace by using discriminatory language. In accord with the principles and linguistic strategies of the "Criteria for the Evaluation of Inclusive Language Translations of Scriptural Texts Proposed for Liturgical Use" (hereafter, CEILT) this translation attempts to "facilitate the full, conscious and active participation of all members of the church, women and men, in worship" (CEILT, no. 13).

Specifically, the generic "he" of the psalms and canticles is translated variously according to the organizing metaphors and internal shifts of person, number and voice manifested in a particular text. Thus in context it may be rendered "I" or "we," "you" or "they" (see CEILT, no. 23).

Furthermore, words no longer understood as inclusive terms, such as "man" or "men," "sons," "brothers" or "brethren," and "forefathers," are avoided (CEILT, nos. 18–19), except where demanded by a particular context. Thus, psalms and canticles that refer to historic males, females and institutions continue to do so in this translation, as in the specific reference to the king in Psalm 72, and to the king, queen, and inheritance customs of Psalm 45:

> *Your sons will inherit*
> *the throne your fathers held. (v. 17)*

Likewise, when the feminine personification of Zion (and the accompanying implicit feminization of the chosen people relative to a divine masculine) is integral to the imagery and meaning of the psalm, this translation honors the operative convention. Thus, Psalm 87:5 is rendered, "Zion mothered each and every one"; without this metaphor, there is no psalm.

This translation also addresses the problem of naming God and has followed the direction of the CEILT, no. 26:

> *Great care should be taken in translations of the*
> *names of God and in the use of pronouns referring to*
> *God. While it would be inappropriate to attribute*
> *gender to God as such, the revealed word of God con-*
> *sistently uses a masculine reference for God. It may*
> *sometimes be useful, however, to repeat the name of*
> *God, as used earlier in the text, rather than to use the*
> *masculine pronoun in every case. But care must be*
> *taken that the repetition not become tiresome.*

In order to deal with direct references to God's name, several strategies have been developed and employed in this translation: (1) The approach to the rendering of the Tetragrammaton YHWH has been discussed above in Section I. (2) Some of the more pervasive and important titles of God, such as "Lord," "King," "Shepherd," are usually retained because they have significant historical and theological resonances that would otherwise be lost. (3) Wherever possible, masculine pronouns are not used to refer to God. Instead: (a) the name itself might be repeated or a synonym provided ("God" or "the Lord"); (b) judging from internal shifts of grammatical person manifested in a particular text, the third person ("he") might be absorbed into a continuous second-person ("you") form throughout the entire psalm or canticle (CEILT, no. 23); (c) or, most commonly, the linguistic structure is arranged in idiomatic English such that the need for a pronominal expression never arises. (4) Finally, this translation seeks to highlight vividly the metaphors of the original texts that reveal God as recognizably personal: a God who acts and whose self is revealed by action. Thus, the verbs attributed to God in this translation, as in the source texts, are strikingly anthropomorphic: a playful God "rides the clouds" (Psalm 68:5); a providential God "blocks the plans of nations" (Psalm 33:10), but "steadies the faithful" (Psalm 37:23); an angry God seethes (Psalm 78:21), and bellows (Psalm 18:16), while a compassionate God "keeps a loving eye" on the faithful (Psalm 33:18), "enfolds" them "with tender care" (Psalm 103:4), and "stands by victims" (Psalm 109:31). Yet the mystery of God's existence remains: a personal existence that embraces and yet transcends gendered human existence (see CEILT, no. 28). Thus, in this rendering as in the original, God is figured "like a king" (Psalm 95:3), "a warrior" (Psalm 78:65), but also "a nesting bird" (Psalm 91:4); God "fathers" (Deuteronomy 32:6, Tobit 13:4), but can love "like a mother" (Psalm 106:46).

CONCLUSION

The aim of this lively poetry crafted especially for the contemporary liturgical assembly is to make the psalter sing the church into a new recognition of the mystery of God still at work in daily life. If the translations have any value, and if composers set them imaginatively for the communities they serve, they will lead to a more vital manifestation of that eternal mystery.

THE DESIGN

The motive in the design of this book is balance. Every page has been tailored to suggest a visual center and to create a graceful presentation of these texts.

We have intended to produce this book in the spirit of fine illuminated manuscripts, giving much attention to the quality of the materials as well as to the crafts of type and design. The typeface is Minion, a contemporary face inspired by classic old style faces; it was designed by Robert Slimbach and released in 1992. The patient, exacting typesetting was done by Jim Mellody-Pizzato. Pages were printed by Congress Printing Company of Chicago on 70 pound Somerset Matte Text. Casebound editions were bound at Zonne Bookbinders, Inc., of Chicago.

Kerry Perlmutter

THE ART

No matter the categories, themes or moods we devise, the psalm will not be defined in one image. Each ancient poem bears a myriad of images, sounds, movements and moods. This only grows richer in the ways these words have been sung and prayed in so many voices and situations. Each of us then echoes the voice embodied in the psalm and thus broadens the possibilities for imagery even more. The words are too tempting to leave them without images, but how to offer any visual equivalent? Image as respite can be one way.

The works on these pages are monotypes. Black etching ink is wiped from a plate with brush, cloth and palette knife to create or to "find" an image. In the transformation from ink plate to paper there is an element of surprise where mystery appropriately enters.

Landscape, objects in nature, shelter, phenomena and energy, mystery and people: these are foundations for the imagery. The scale runs from close to vast. The placement for the art at varying intervals is intended to be that respite, that invitation to contemplate, a visual meditation wherein we catch our breath between these sweeping, all-embracing words of prayer.

Linda Ekstrom